K13 Remembered
An Untold Story

Keith Hall

Cover: The K13 graves at the Faslane cemetery

All royalties raised from the sale of this book will be donated to
the Submarine Heritage Centre Helensburgh

ISBN: 9781731559517

PREAMBLE

The British submarine K13 flooded and sank in Gare Loch, Scotland, in the early afternoon of Monday 29 January 1917 shortly after her final acceptance trial dive. Of the eighty men on board, thirty-two people lost their lives. The West of Scotland branch of the Submariners Association have been organising the K13 Memorial Service for the past 35 years. January 2017 saw the 100th anniversary of the sinking and as part of the branch's preparations I did some research into the accident.

The circumstances of the submarine's loss were investigated very promptly, 14 days after the rescue, but for mainly security reasons nothing was published at the time and very little was released officially after the war. The Board of Inquiry (B O I) was set up to investigate the circumstances of the loss and laid the blame for this accident solely on Lt Arthur Lane, the vessel's engineer.

The minutes of the Board of Inquiry were particularly troubling, containing many inconsistencies, and the more I looked into it, the more I became convinced that the Board's findings were wrong. The seemingly casual way the Board of Inquiry came to its verdict was unsettling and only deepened my conviction that the Board were mistaken. I found it difficult to believe that Lt Lane would allow his submarine to dive with the Boiler Room intakes open, as the Board concluded. I am more than aware that people are capable of doing the most stupid things, often with, seemingly, total disregard for the consequences of their actions or their own or others safety. But nobody is more than aware of the dangers a submariner faces than the submariner himself, he would never have dived his submarine with the intakes open.

The men and officers in a submarine know that their lives depend on their crew mates, who may endanger the vessel by a thoughtless action or by ignorance, and ultimately kill the crew. In a submarine, an officer or a man's ability for his job is the only real measure by which he is judged and the bar is set very high.

This and a re-examination of the Board's minutes led me to question the validity and accuracy of the verdict. My unrest was further magnified by an examination of the available documentation regarding the accident, these tended to highlight more inconsistencies. These document were:

A paper published in Marine Engineer and Naval Architect written by J Foster Petree MIMECH.E. MRINA. He highlights certain inconsistencies between the Hillhouse Report and Everitt's description of the K13 accident, but more importantly, he questions how the flooding of the Boiler Room caused the whole of the submarine to flood. The second document was The Hillhouse Report. Mr P.A. Hillhouse (later Professor), the Naval Architect from Fairfield, gave a lecture to the Greenock Association of Engineers and Shipbuilders in 1918 on the K13 accident, this was presumably given with The Admiralty's approval. As Mr Hillhouse was a survivor of the accident, this report must be considered factual. And no book about K Class submarines could be written without reference to Don Everitt's book, 'The K Boats'. He was a professional journalist who had researched the subject thoroughly and succeeded in gathering a great deal of scattered and personal information that was not generally available.

My thoughts eventually coalesced into this book and it would be fair to say that the aim was to clear Lt Lane's name and restore his reputation. Something he wasn't able to do himself as he tragically lost his life with the sinking of the submarine. I hope the book will convince readers of Lt Lane's innocence. Much of this has to be conjecture and or speculation but I would argue this is not too much different to the original Board of Inquiry.

To help put this period into context for readers, chapter 1 is an overview of early British development and the policies behind it, a description of the K class submarines. This is followed by a review of submarine crew training. Chapter 2 covers the actual accident and lists casualties and survivors. It also details the actual accident position. Chapter 3 is a word for word transcript of the Board of Inquiry and Chapter 4 reviews this, highlighting inconsistencies and stating the counter arguments. Chap 5 presents the reader with an alternative scenario which calls into doubt the Board's findings, essentially, what I think happened. Chapter 6 sums up the previous chapters in essence, it states the case for Lt Lane's defense. The Epilogue is the history of the K13 memorial service, which is held annually in January at the Faslane cemetery.

I have purposely avoided including a Glossary and I explain the abbreviations in the text, avoiding the need for the reader to flip backwards and forwards through the book. For a similar reason I have not included footnotes or references. Readers requiring further information should refer to the texts in the bibliography.

I believe the living owe it to those who can no longer speak, to tell their story for them. I would like to think that this book does.

Contents

ACKNOWLEDGMENTS

Many people have contributed to this book. I am grateful to Gerry McFeely, for allowing me access to his Centennial Notes and as always, his friendly advice and support. David Piggett for sharing and giving me permission to use his extensive notes on the K Class submarines and answering and putting up with my endless queries.

Barrie Downer for his help with the biographical information and supplying me with information from his extensive database, particularly his notes on early submarine training. I am very grateful for his seemingly endless patience. Also George Malcolmson from the Royal Naval Submarine Museum for searching and supplying material from the Museum's archives.

Special thanks to Ron Rietveld, Garry Luxford and Chris Leggett for answering my interminable questions and the much-needed engineering advice. It must have been very hard work keeping a 'medic' on track. Andy Griffin from Castrol Technical Support for shedding some very necessary light on the waxing process.

I am indebted to the following for their assistance and support in helping me complete this book, Keith S Hall. Also John and Anne Lenting and Ron Rietveld for reading the fledgling manuscript and their helpful suggestions. Adrian Rietveld for the initial art work on the book cover.

Particularly thanks to José Piët for her encouragement, helpful suggestions and extensive and very thorough proofreading of the manuscript during its evolution. And for taking the emotive cover photograph.

All MOD pictures and quotes from official documents are reproduced under the Governments Open Licence scheme. Contains public sector information licensed under the Open Government Licence v3.0.

I must stress any mistakes in the book are due to my inattentiveness, all the people involved couldn't have been more helpful and showed a remarkable degree of patience towards me and my endless and often inane questions;

CHAPTER 1

K-CLASS SUBMARINES

PART 1

EARLY BRITISH SUBMARINE DEVELOPMENT

The design that would eventually evolve into the K-class submarines was first proposed by Sir Eustace d'Eyncourt in 1913 in response to an Admiralty request for a new class of submarine that could operate with the surface fleet. It was intended that these submarines would sail ahead of the fleet and try to get behind the German High Seas Fleet and ambush it as it was forced to retreat from the superior British Grand Fleet. Although they had only been in service for a relatively short period of 12 years, these new vessels had already caused some division within the Naval community.

In the late 19th century submarines were being built by several nations, although none of these countries' naval establishments supported these early vessels. As far as the British Navy were concerned they didn't seem to pose a threat to the mighty British fleets, they were very slow and what weapons they could use were ineffective. That aside, the Admiralty kept a weathered eye on these developments. In 1898, Captain Henry Jackson, the British naval attaché in Paris, had been instructed to report on French submarine developments. He witnessed trials of the privately developed, Le Goubet. This was a small 11-ton submersible that was designed to be carried on board a warship. In January 1899 he informed the Admiralty that 270 ton experimental submarine Gustave Zédé had conducted a torpedo attack on the battleship Magenta. In June 1900, the French commissioned the steam and electric powered Narval. This submarine had what was to become the classic double-hull design, with a pressure hull covered by an outer light free flooding casing. These 200-ton vessels had a range of over 100 miles underwater. In 1904 The French submarine Aigrette introduced a further improvement by using a diesel instead of a petrol engine when running on the surface.

In January 1900, the British naval attaché in Washington, Captain Charles Ottley, reported that the US government was considering purchasing a submarine designed by the Irish inventor John Holland. Captain Ottley sent the Admiralty the US Navy's reports on the boat's performance and a set of blueprints.

Although the Board of Admiralty felt some of the French reports were exaggerated and rejected further reports that said the French had ordered up to a dozen submarines, they saw fit to instruct the torpedo school to investigate means of combatting submarines. First Sea Lord Walter Kerr and the Controller, Rear Admiral Arthur Knyvet-Wilson, were convinced of the need to obtain a submarine so the navy could investigate its capabilities and methods could be prepared to combat the submarine threat.

The Board of Admiralty was slowly reassessing its opinion of these craft and now considered that perhaps they could be used offensively as opposed to playing a purely defensive role. This, in part, explains why the Admiralty delayed becoming involved in any submarine development program. Another reason was that they were trying to avoid an 'arms race' with foreign navies. Conversely, once those navies did begin serious submarine building programs, the Admiralty had little choice but to follow and start its own submarine construction program. Added to this, Admiral Fisher, who, at this time, was in command of the Mediterranean Fleet, asked the Admiralty for instructions on the best defence against submarines. He suggested that defensive mines might be suitable. He also felt that there might be a strong possibility he might be required to fight the French.

In response to this, the Admiralty felt that the best way to address these concerns and meet the requirements was to start its own submarine construction program. Between 1901 and 1903, the Royal Navy ordered five Holland-class submarines, and providing the various trials that the boats were involved in were successful, further orders would be placed.

John Philip Holland, was born 29 February 1840, in Liscannor, County Clare, Ireland, (he died 12 August 1914, in Newark, N.J., U.S.). He built his first model submarine in 1876, then, four years later, built a full size one. This was intended to be used by the Fenian Brotherhood, the American counterpart to the Irish Republican Brotherhood, against the British. The construction and

5

launching of the submarine in 1881 by the Delamater Iron Company in New York was funded by the Fenians' Skirmishing Fund. Officially, this craft was known as Holland Boat No. II. The role of the Fenians in its funding led the New York Sun newspaper to call it the Fenian Ram. This was followed by several unsuccessful designs until 1896, when he designed the Holland Type VI submarine. One of his last inventions was an apparatus designed to enable the crew to escape from sunken submarine

Despite his anti-British leanings, he still found it in himself to sell his submarine designs to the British. Money, it seems, is able to disentangle many a moral dilemma and smooth an uneasy conscience. No British shipbuilder had any experience in submarine construction, so the Admiralty began negotiations with the Holland Torpedo Boat Company and Vickers Ltd; a major shipbuilder for the Admiralty. It was agreed that The Electric Boat Company, who purchased the rights from Holland's company, would license Vickers to build submarines in Britain.

The design chosen by the Royal Navy was an untested, improved version of the original Holland design, powered by a new 180 hp petrol engine. The keel of the first boat was laid down 4 February 1901. In order to keep the boat's construction secret, she was assembled in a building labelled "Yacht Shed", and the parts that had to be fabricated in the general yard were marked "for pontoon No 1". Despite the secrecy surrounding the project, the story that Vickers were building submarines was leaked by a Glasgow newspaper in February, this was confirmed by the Admiralty a month later in March. She was launched on 2 October 1901 and dived for the first time, in an enclosed basin, on 20 March 1902. Her sea trials began in April 1902. The Admiralty had hoped to keep these submarines a secret, only a few senior officers knew of the build program. In part, this resulted in the myth that the Admiralty was not taking any interest in submarines.

Arnold Forster, Secretary of State for War, continued to press for more submarines to be built, he was of the opinion that the navy either needed a large number or none. Although William Palmer, 2nd Earl of Selborne, who was First Lord of the Admiralty, agreed, both were opposed by the Sea Lords. It was finally agreed that three submarines a year would be ordered. This was the minimum number needed to enable Vickers to maintain their specialist submarine construction team. Although it was known that the French design was technically superior to the Holland boats that had just been ordered, the Admiralty had credible alternative at this time.

When the first British submarines and their tender, HMS Hazard, arrived at Portsmouth in September 1902, they were immediately banished to the far reaches of the harbour, amongst the prison hulks and quarantine vessels. This was due to fears about their petrol engines. They became known as the "First Submarine Flotilla" and was commanded by Captain Reginald Bacon. He was appointed Inspecting Captain of Submarines, his task being to manage the development of the submarines. He was a technically minded officer who had served on surface torpedo boats. On taking up this appointment he noted the Holland class submarines were inferior to the current French design and they would be unable to operate on the surface in anything other than fair weather. The submarines only had a limited underwater range of 20 miles. He recommended that the designs of Holland four and five should be altered to improve their sea keeping qualities. The Admiralty were of the opinion that the designer, the Holland company, would not allow changes to their design and would not take responsibility for any problems caused by these unauthorised design changes. Therefore, they ordered one submarine of a new design, which was the A1. Bacon was also of the opinion that 3 to 5 submarines would provide a very effective defense against any enemy ships attempting to operate near a harbour where the submarines were based.

At this time, including the crews of the depot ship HMS Thames and the tender HMS Hazard, the total strength of the newly formed service was just over a hundred men.

As mentioned, the primary concern for the traditional navy was how to effectively deal with these new-fangled vessels. To this end, in November 1902, tests were carried out to determine the vulnerability of the Holland class submarines to underwater explosions. These experiments showed that the submarine was safe from a 200-lb gun cotton charge when it was exploded 80 yards from the submarine. As there was no way of detecting the submarine's location once it had submerged, it was relatively immune to attack. In fact, it was felt that the attacking destroyers were more at risk, as they could blow their own sterns dropping the new depth charges.

A more pressing problem was the submarines' reliability, initially they had serious mechanical problems. In 1903 the flotilla attempted a surface passage round the Isle of Wight; four of the boats broke down before they had covered 4 miles. On 3 March 1903 Holland 1 suffered an explosion that resulted in four injuries.

On 24 October, 1905 three Holland submarines sailed from Portsmouth after Russian ships mistakenly sank a number of British fishing vessels in the Dogger Bank. They were recalled before they could get into a position to attack.

After the Hollands, the Royal Navy embarked on an extensive submarine building program, initially the A-class. Between 1902 – 1905 13 new boats were built and there was considerable variation amongst the boats. Generally they were around 100 feet long and displaced approximately 200 tons submerged. The first, A1, initially ordered as Holland No.6, was launched in July 1902, the last, A13, in April 1905. They were powered underwater by electric motors and used petrol engines for surface propulsion. A13 had an experimental 500 bhp Vickers diesel engine, which was unreliable. They had two 18-inch torpedo tubes with four torpedoes. A1 had 1 tube and 3 torpedoes.

These were followed by the B-class, a class of 11 submarines, also built by Vickers in Barrow-in-Furness between 1904 and 1906. One of the class was sunk by a collision in 1912, but the rest served in World War I. Three boats protected the transfer of the British Expeditionary Force to France in 1914 but were soon relegated to local defence and training duties. Six submarines were in the Mediterranean when the war began and were quickly sent to the Dardanelles to prevent a breakout by the German battlecruiser SMS Goeben and the light cruiser SMS Breslau into the Eastern Mediterranean. B11 was operating in the Dardanelles in December 1914 and sank the elderly Turkish ironclad Mesudiye. The older B-class submarines were withdrawn to Malta in 1915 as newer submarines became available for the Dadanelles blockade. Later they were transferred to Venice when Italy entered the war. While stationed here, B10 became the first submarine to be sunk by air attack in 1916. By late 1916, as they were no longer considered operational, they were transferred back to Malta. In mid-1917 they were converted to surface patrol boats and used to patrol the Otranto Barrage. They proved to be unreliable and were soon sent back to Malta where they were finally paid off. Only B3 was still in commission when the war ended, primarily because it was being used for experimental work and she also served as a target to train anti-submarine forces.

The C-class submarines marked the end of designs that were essentially English versions of the Holland class. They were also the last submarines to be powered by a petrol engine. Thirty-eight were built between 1906 and 1910. With limited endurance and only a ten percent reserve of buoyancy over their surface displacement, they were poor surface vessels, although their spindle shaped hull made for good underwater performance when compared to other existing British submarines. Despite these drawbacks, three C-Class submarines sailed to Hong Kong in 1911, to join the China Station. This successful voyage showed the potential of these small rudimentary craft.

The D class marked a radicle change of direction and purpose for the Submarine Service. Between 1908–1912 eight submarines were built. They were nearly twice the size of the previous C-

Class submarines, they had a crew of twenty-five, and were intended for patrolling enemy waters for extended periods. They were the first British submarines with diesel engines. They had three torpedo tubes and some had a deck gun.

Captain Keyes, who took over as Inspecting Captain, 14 November, 1910 and on 31 August, 1912, was appointed to HMS Dolphin as Commodore, Second Class, in charge of the Submarine Service. He blamed Fisher for the state of the service, arguing that as Vickers had been given the monopoly for submarine building in Britain, he had little option but to look for new designs abroad. Since 1904 Vickers had the exclusive rights to the patents of John Holland. Perhaps because of this arrangement, Britain had not really produced an original submarine design, while on the continent many countries were producing their own submarines to their own design. Keyes also blamed Vickers for not working to their full capacity despite orders from the navy. As a result, three Italian designed submarines were ordered from Scotts of Greenock on the Clyde and four French submarines from Armstrong Whitworth. His rational was questionable as the Vickers agreement had ended. He also criticised Fisher for ordering too many coastal submarines, which caused a shortage of oversea submarines. A questionable claim as his, recently ordered, continental submarines were of no greater range or size than those built by Fisher. In effect it could be argued that Keyes wasted limited resources on a large number of foreign designs or adaptations of these designs. Many warned against this rational, reasoning that it would be impossible to get the equipment to complete the builds should war break out. Several of the submarines were delayed because of this. In 1913 Keyes alleged they were only building coastal submarines, not the overseas ones, he maintained, the navy needed.

The D class were followed by fifty-eight E class submarines. These were built between 1912-1916, two of them were for the Royal Australian Navy. They were bigger and more sophisticated than previous classes and became the mainstay of the wartime submarine fleet. The class primarily served in the North Sea and the Baltic, where some served with Russian ships in Russian coastal waters before their crews scuttled the submarines to avoid them falling into the hands of the Communists. Also, some operated against the Turks. The E class went through several design modifications as submarine technology improved.

The British L-class submarine eventually replaced the E class. These were originally planned under the emergency war program, although they came into service too late to make any significant contribute to the war effort. They served throughout the 1920s and the majority were scrapped in the 1930s but three remained operational as training boats during World War II. The last three were scrapped in 1946 after a long and distinguished career. Parts of uncompleted L-class submarines were used for the Yugoslav Hrabri-class submarines.

Originally designed as coastal submarines, the three F class submarines were built between 1913–1917. All three of the class survived the war and were then used as training boats based in Campbelltown.

Keyes eventually requested an oversea submarine design from Vickers and Scotts. Vickers proposed a submarine double the size of the biggest submarine currently in service with a range of 5300 miles. Although the Scotts design was much smaller, the company made the radical suggestion, that in view of the poor reliability of the Fiat engines, which they built under license, steam turbines should be used to power the submarine. Keyes ordered one of each design, the Vickers boat being named Nautilus, while the Scotts boat was named Swordfish and its usual mode of propulsion was kept secret.

The S-class submarines were built by Scotts, Greenock just before World War I and were based on the Italian Laurenti submarines. Three vessels were constructed, all of them were transferred to the Italian Navy in October 1915.

The W-class submarines were built as experimental boats. They were based on a French Schneider-Laubeuf design and 4 boats were built between 1914 – 1915. W3 and W4 were greatly modified to reflect the Royal Navy's requirements. These alterations also helped overcome some of the problems inherent with 'off the shelf' designs. Apart from problems with habitability the class were generally good submarines. All 4 of the W-class submarine were transferred to the Italian Navy in August 1916.

4 V-class submarines were built by Vickers, Barrow in Furness during World War I in response to Scotts building the S-class and Armstrong Whitworth building the W class.

The 3 submarines of the F-class were built by Chatham, White and Thornycroft. F2 had a MAN diesel, the two others Vickers ones. The battery comprised 128 Exide cells. Two additional ones were ordered in 1914 but later cancelled. These small submarines saw little service.

The G-class submarines were designed by the Admiralty in response to a rumour that the Germans were building double-hulled submarines for overseas duties. 14 submarines were built between 1915 and 1917. G1 to G5 were built at Chatham Dockyard, G6 & G7 by Armstrong Whitworth, G8 to G13 by Vickers, and G14 by Scotts on the Clyde. A fifteen submarine was ordered from Samuel White's yard at Cowes, Isle of Wight, but cancelled. The submarines had a partial double hull but this did little to improve the slow diving times that were common at this time. Most of the class had their bows raised during the war to increase buoyancy and improve seakeeping. They had a crew of 30.

The H-class submarines were Holland 602 type submarines, 44 were constructed between 1915 and 1919. They were designed to mine the German coast and attack German submarines operating in British waters. Regardless of their cramped interiors and lack of a deck gun on some submarines, they were very popular with their crews. After the war many were retained for training purpose. Although outdated by the outbreak of the Second World War, they were nevertheless retained in training and coastal warfare roles.

Seven J class submarines were developed by the Royal Navy prior to the First World War in response to claims that Germany was developing submarines that were fast enough to operate alongside surface fleets. Six were completed during mid-1916, a seventh entered service at the end of 1917.
Although larger and more powerful than previous British submarines, they did not have the speed to keep up with surface vessels. During the war HMS J6 was lost to friendly fire. After the war, the six surviving submarines were transferred to the Royal Australian Navy.

M-submarines were a class of 3 diesel-electric submarines built between 1917 and 1918. They had 12-inch (305 mm) gun which was mounted in a turret forward of the conning tower. Due to the limitations imposed on submarine armament by the Washington Naval Conference, M2 and M3 had their guns removed. M2 was converted to carry a small seaplane and M3 was made into a minelayer.

A lot of the pre-war naval budget was spent on the "Dreadnought race", and as a result, submarine construction declined between 1910 and 1914. This required a period of increased production when the war started in August 1914 to enable the Navy to 'catch up' with the Germans. Also, German U-boat successes against both merchant shipping and Royal Navy warships in the first few months of the war, promoted the view that the German submarine was a very real threat to the dominance of the Grand Fleet in the North Sea.

Although it might be possible to accuse certain senior officers of being slow in recognising the full potential of the submarine, very little was actually done to hinder their development and by the start of World War One, the Royal Navy had the world's largest submarine service. This comprised of 72 B, C and D class submarines, 15 were oceangoing, the rest capable of coastal patrols. Most of these were stationed in Naval Bases around the British coast but 6 B class submarines were stationed in the Mediterranean and 3 C boats at Hong Kong.

PART 2

POLITICS OF SUBMARINE
DEVELOPMENT

In many European countries in the late eighteenth century, the idea that submarine warfare was unacceptable, even morally offensive, was common. France, in particular, thought that submarines could not meet the accepted rules of war. There was a general feeling that there was something contemptible about underwater weapons, be they mines, torpedoes or submarines. Although unproven, they were thought to be secretive, and destructive, the fact that they were impossible to detect, made them difficult to counter and impossible to escape from. In 1900 many British naval officers would probably have agreed that the Royal Navy, indeed, the whole world, would be a better place without them. In fact, in 1900, the First Lord of Admiralty, George Goschen, stated;

"The Admiralty are not prepared to take any steps in regards to submarines, because this vessel is the weapon of the weaker nation. If, however, this vessel can be rendered practical, the nation which possesses it, will cease to be weak and will became really powerful. More than any other nation we should have to fear the attack of submarines."

This view was not shared by all British politicians. After the November general election in 1900, the new Parliamentary Secretary to the Admiralty Board was Hugh Oakley Arnold-Forster. As a backbencher he had criticised Goschen for not recognising that the submarine was a potential, viable weapon. Once in post, he found that the Admiralty had been evaluating submarine designs, in secret, for a number of years. Despite this, he was concerned that the navy was trailing the French in development and construction of these craft. The first British submarine, being built by Vickers, wouldn't be in service until October 1901. To improve the situation, he suggested that other companies should be involved in the building program. This was strongly opposed by Vice Admiral Archibald Douglas, the Second Sea Lord and Admiral Wilson. The main reason for their stance was that they thought it would encourage smaller navies to purchase submarines of their own and this, they felt, would not be in the best interests of the Royal Navy. They thought that any measures that would delay submarine development should be taken and the navy must investigate any methods that might offer some protection against these small craft.

So perhaps, not surprisingly, the establishment of the Royal Navy's Submarine Service, in the early 1900s, was not welcomed by the majority of the traditional Victorian Navy. These small craft and their scruffy crews were a complete anathema to the smartly uniformed officers of the conventional big-ship navy. Their arrival was controversial, incredibly divisive and the ensuing debate about their capabilities and usefulness was notable for its bias and its generally ill-informed nature. This was primarily due to the fact that before the war very little was known about the capabilities of the submarine. This was not particularly surprising as they had not been in action since the American Civil War some 50 years previously. Understandably, in the absence of any current combat experience, the navy assessed these craft by conducting a series of exercises and war games. The aim was to reveal possible strategies and demonstrate potential roles for these new craft. These annual manoeuvres should have given a far better understanding of the capabilities of the submarine. Unfortunately, this was not the case, primarily due to the fact that the exercises tended to be unrealistic. This, in turn, produced unreliable data, which did little to enlighten the debate. Also, the exercises were organised to confirm the efficacy of the current policies and strategies and did little to help evaluate the new underwater weapon. Another factor which made it difficult to accurately evaluate the performance of the submarine was the fact that anything that might hazard the submarine or her crew was not allowed, safety was paramount. These annual manoeuvres should have given a far better understanding of the capabilities of the submarine. Before submarines took part in these exercises, the only method of assessment were the war games played by officers attending the Greenwich War Course. These games probably gave an even more unrealistic view than the sea going exercises. The Greenwich rules, also known as Jane's Rules, were naïve and impractical and did little to reflect the submarine's capabilities. Under the rules, it took submarines 30 minutes to reload after firing a torpedo, and when the submarine was underwater, the captain had to sit with his back to the other players, watching the unfolding events through, as the Rules stipulated, "a small fragment of looking-glass, not exceeding half-an-inch in diameter".

This lack of information about the submarine's abilities, caused views to become very polarised, you were either for or against these novel vessels. Admiral Fisher, the First Sea Lord, was probably the most enthusiastic advocate of the submarine. It is more than likely that without his patronage the submarine service would have developed in quite a different manner, almost certainly not as many submarines would have been built and it's unlikely they would have been developed beyond the coastal defence role. As early as 1904 Fisher could see the submarine would revolutionise naval warfare and he became a very vocal champion of these new-fangled craft. He felt that they would replace the Dreadnoughts as the Fleet's capital ships. He saw submarines as a symbol of change, a change that he was the champion of. Unfortunately, he was a self-opinionated man with a belligerent personality and he made enemies both within the Royal Navy and in politics. He clashed with Lord Beresford, who commanded the Channel Fleet and he found himself increasingly isolated within the Navy's hierarchy and retired from the Navy in 1910. Before this, he managed to lay the foundations of the Submarine Service regardless of the strong opposition from fellow Naval Officers and politicians. They referred to him as a lunatic and the submarines were called his playthings. He was even forced to hide the funding for them in the naval estimates

The naval traditionalists, who were opposed to these new vessels, shouldn't be thought of as non-thinking die-hards, they did not disagree with the fact that the submarine could become a powerful weapon, they just pointed out that it would take a considerable amount of time to reach this state. For example, Admiral Sir

Reginald Custance, a former Director of Intelligence, thought the submarine may have some value, but as there was very little data available on how they would perform in battle, their use and efficacy would probably be exaggerated. This was undoubtedly compounded by the fact that the designers of the submarines often overstated the effectiveness of their inventions. The traditionists argued that they were not considered the weapon of a major naval power and the fledgling submarines were viewed with a degree of cynicism as was the entire concept of submarine warfare. There were moral objections and several Admirals were even calling for captured submarine crews to be hung. Speaking in 1901, Admiral Sir Arthur Wilson, then Controller of the Navy, viewed the submarine as 'underhand, unfair and damned un-English'. The cost and effectiveness of using these novel and unproven craft was questioned and they were considered little more than harbour protection vessels. Admiral Beresford, who referred to submarines as 'Fisher's playthings', said of the submarine flotilla after exercises in 1908, that the exercises "were really planned to show the utility of submarines." He was convinced that the navy was abandoning the only true and traditional policy of the British i.e. to find out the enemy in Blue Water and destroy him, and that the General has been informed that the submarines will prevent invasion and put down any enemy even in their own ports". He said this was totally wrong and in a recent exercise submarines were within 120 miles of him for three days and did nothing. Even as late as 1914 he was still of the opinion that the submarine was an essentially defensive weapon that could not defend herself and was best operated by day in clear weather.

In fact, the second Inspecting Captain of Submarines, Captain Edgar Lees, went so far as to state,

"The British Navy has never wanted submarine boats, but a share in their evolution has been of late forced upon us by other nations."

It was felt that there was no way these early submarines, with their low speeds, very limited capabilities and ineffective armament could do anything to complement the traditional Nelsonian view the navy had of itself, where big fleets with large numbers of ships, fought for control of the seas. They saw the Royal Navy was an instrument for all-out attack.

As late as 1914 Admiral William Henderson was still of the opinion that,

"Even if a submarine should work by a miracle, it will never be used. No country in this world would ever use such a vicious and petty form of warfare."

Apart from naval traditionists, the First Sea Lord had several other opponents. A number of pressure groups, including the Imperial Maritime League, and a large number of newspapers didn't share his enthusiasm for the submarine. Also, Fisher's habit of branding anybody who dared to disagree with his views as an enemy, alienated many of his colleagues and the Navy's united front, it presented to the public, was somewhat dented. Even H.G Wells entered the debate and opined,

"I must confess that my imagination refuses to see any sort of submarine doing anything but suffocating its crew and floundering at sea."

Views, throughout the navy in general, were slowly changing, in part due to the attitudes, dedication, enthusiasm and professionalism of the submarine's Commanding Officers and their crews. The submarines reliability continued to improve and those who had observed the submarines during exercises were becoming convinced of their usefulness. Advocates of the submarine lead by Admiral Fisher were firmly of the opinion that submarines would be the battleships of the future. Perhaps a strange stance considering that Fisher had just introduced the Dreadnoughts. Admiral Sir Percy Scott's letter in the Times 15 December 1913.

"The introduction of vessels which swim under water as, in my opinion, entirely done away with the utility of the ships that swim on top of the water."

Admiral Sir William May openly derided Custance's old-school views accusing him of underestimating the submarine's potential. Later in 1904, he thought that within a few years, once the submarines were true seagoing vessels, they would mark a real revolution in naval warfare. The commander of the Grand Fleet at the outbreak of war, Admiral George Ashley Callaghan, wrote a paper on anti-submarine warfare. He concluded that

"the value of the submarine as a weapon, both of offence and defence, is enormous."

An article appeared in the winter edition of the Naval Review (1913-1914) supporting Fisher's views. In it the author criticised the current approach, referring to it as an 'ostrich policy.'

Even Admiral Custance began to think that submarines, "are being exploited along entirely the wrong lines. My view is that if a weapon of this sort is developed with an eye for its use in offensive warfare, its use in the defensive will be covered, but that the reverse does not hold". Wilson considered that the limited range of existing submarines meant they would only be able to operate in French waters, whereas if further developed, could become a weapon to threaten British home ports. He recognised the potential of the submarine to prevent maritime trade, which was essential to the survival of an island nation like Britain.

At this time, several of the Admiralty's senior "futurists," among them the Inspector Captain of Submarines Commodore Roger Keyes, had suggested an idea that would greatly increase the role of the submarine force when operating with the Grand Fleet. They proposed that if several high-speed submarines in conjunction with the cruiser screen, sailing ahead of the main battle force, they would be in the ideal position to submerge and attack the approaching enemy fleet before they could engage the British fleet. To be able to do this would require a submarine that had a surface speed of 21 knots, regardless of the sea conditions in the North Sea. Both Admirals Sir John Jellicoe, the Grand Fleet's Commander-in-Chief and Sir David Beatty, the Battle Cruiser Force Commander, endorsed this proposal and emphasised the urgent need for a high-speed "fleet submarine" to achieve this.

Sir Eustance Tennyson-d'Eyncourt, the Director of Naval Construction, was convinced the only way to meet this requirement was to use steam turbines. Numerous naval officers, among them many from the submarine community, were openly critical about this. Unsurprisingly, Fisher waded into the debate and in June 1913 he famously wrote that oil powered engines would govern all sea fighting and that steam engines in submarines was a mistake.

In the spring of that year, Tennyson-d'Eyncourt produced another design for a large submarine powered by steam turbines. It would be some 338 feet long and displace 1700 tons. Its engines would give it a surface speed of 24 knots, it would have 4 21 inch bow torpedo tubes and 4 beam torpedo tubes. It would have 2 guns mounted on the casing. At a conference called for by the Third Sea Lord, which was attended by Keyes and d'Eyncourt, it was agreed not to proceed with this design. The reasons being, the great increase in size over current submarines, the use of steam turbines and the problems of controlling such a large submarine underwater. Up until October 1914 there were no developments that would cause Fisher to alter his opinion. The numerous delays and problems completing the steam powered Swordfish at Greenock only reinforced his view.

At this time, most Cabinet Ministers and the majority of senior naval officers were of the opinion that submarines were slow, not particularly seaworthy and as they couldn't keep up with the Fleet, their only use was in the coastal defence role. When Fisher warned, in 1912 and early 1914, that German submarines would attack and sink Allied merchant ships without warning, Churchill dismissed his statement. Even when Admiral Percy Scott wrote in the Times, pointing out that airplanes and submarines had rendered the battleship obsolete. Churchill and other politicians were still unconvinced, that was until a U boat had entered the Firth of Forth, 1 September 1914, and sailed as far as the railway bridge. Four days later the flotilla leader HMS Pathfinder was torpedoed in the Channel. Then, 22 September, U9 sank the British cruisers Aboukir, Hogue and Cressy, while patrolling the Broad Fourteens, a region of the southern North Sea. She fired four of her torpedoes, reloading while submerged. To compound matters, 1st October 1914, the Grand Fleet was forced to sail from its anchorage in Scapa Flow when U boats were, mistakenly, reportedly sighted. At this time the Grand Fleet consisted of approximately 150 ships of which 28 were Dreadnoughts, there were 9 Battlecruisers, 36 armoured and light cruisers and 79 destroyers. The Fleet sailed to Loch Ewe where it anchored for 17 days until it was felt it was safe to return to Scapa Flow.

On 15 October the squadron was on patrol off Aberdeen and HMS Hawke stopped at 9:30 am to pick up mail from her sister ship HMS Endymion. After recovering her boat with the mail, she proceeded at 13 knots, unfortunately without zig-zagging, to regain her station. At 10:30, while out of sight of the rest of the Squadron, she was attacked by U9, which fired a single torpedo, and she quickly capsized. HMS Swift, a destroyer, was dispatched from Scapa Flow to search for survivors. She found one officer and twenty-one men on a life raft, while a boat with a further forty-nine survivors was rescued by a Norwegian steamer. 524 Officers and men had died, there were only 70 survivors. 17th October 1914, again as a result of false U boat sightings, the Fleet sailed to Lough Swilly in Northern Ireland. A U boat had been sighted off Loch Ewe so the Fleet had to find another harbour.

These alarming exploits of the German submarine fleet undoubtedly caused Churchill and Jellico grave concern and those members of the Admiralty who considered submarines to be mere toys, found themselves with some serious rethinking to do. Concerns were further raised when it was rumoured that the Germans were building large, ocean-going submarines, capable of operating on the surface at 22 knots. In mid-October 1914, Churchill wrote to the First Sea Lord querying the current state of the submarine service. He was particularly interested in how many submarines were under construction and what could be done to increase this number, if it was deemed necessary. He was not satisfied with the reply and restated his questions, even more robustly, two weeks later. On October 28, 1914 Churchill sent a memo authorising the use of steam engines to supplement oil engines if it was thought necessary.

30 October 1914, Churchill reappointed Fisher as First Sea Lord. Churchill found him "a veritable volcano of knowledge and of inspiration". Unfortunately, both men had very similar temperaments and this made a disagreement practically unavoidable. It was caused over the Dardanelles campaign, when Churchill wanted to move British warships from the Mediterranean to the Dardanelles. Fisher felt this would weaken the Royal Navy in the Mediterranean Sea and would not support the move and as a result he resigned in May 1915. Fisher was 73 years old when he re-joined the Admiralty. He found the Navy had 12 fewer submarines than when he left in January 1910. He openly blamed Keyes and, for that matter, many other high ranking naval officers, for the mismanagement of and 'damn' mess the service was in. Interestingly, he avoided blaming Churchill, who was in charge of naval building programs during these years.

One of his first tasks was to increase the number of submarines available and within a few days he had placed orders for 38 submarines from 12 companies. A few days later he ordered a further 16, 6 from British yards and 10 from the Bethlehem Steel Corporation of America. There was no shortage of designs to choose from thanks to Keyes's efforts, there were 6 different types. Fisher disregarded these and also ignored Churchill's suggestion regarding steam power and ordered modified versions of the E class that he had commissioned 5 years earlier. The robustness of Fisher's policy was evident in the outstanding war record of the E-class submarines and its derivative, the G class. Keyes's designs actually did very little, the S and W class submarines were sold to Italy as they were unsuitable for northern waters. The V and F classes were not used.

Before the submarines that Fisher had ordered had entered service, seagoing Flag Officers were reporting German submarines with surface speeds in excess of 17 knots. The loss of HMS Formidable to a U boat torpedo attack on New Year's Day 1915, only aggravated the situation. The submarine was reported to have kept up with the battleship in a gale; 547 from a crew of 780 lost their lives as a result of the attack. In response, Fisher ordered the Director of Naval Construction to design a submarine that would have a surface speed in excess of 20 knots. There were no diesel engines available that would enable a submarine to attain the required speed. Once again, d'Eyncourt reaffirmed his view that the only solution was to use steam turbines, he assured, he could then guarantee speeds in excess of 20 knots.

The French steam-driven submarine Archimede was attached to Keyes's submarine command. On 17 December 1915 she was part of a screen with several British submarines in the Helgoland Bight, the idea being to ambush the German battle-cruiser squadron returning to base after shelling Scarborough and Hartlepool. During the evening severe weather damaged the funnel and it couldn't be lowered and due to the bad weather, the Boiler Room began to flood. The crew had to form a bucket chain and only determined bailing saved the submarine. One of the bailers was the submarines British liaison officer, Lieutenant Commander Godfrey Herbert. After two days of continuous bailing the submarine reached Harwich. Fisher used this story to prove to D'Eyncourt that putting funnels and air intakes on a submarine were not a good combination. Fisher would not entertain any more talk of steam powered submarines. Therefore, by the end of January 1915 the constructor department had produced a design that, according to d'Eyncourt, would be capable of 21 knots. This would become known as the J Class and would be powered by 3 E Class diesel engines. Fisher immediately ordered 8 of them from the naval dockyards at Portsmouth, Devonport and Pembroke in Wales. This satisfied the flag officers of the Grand Fleet, who still believed that the fleets should have their own squadrons of submarines, which would be capable of operating with the fleet at its normal operating speed of 21 knots. Not surprisingly, serving submariners certainly didn't share this view, they could see the dangers of trying to maneuver a dived submarine close to a surface ship. Even when surfaced the submarines low profile made them difficult to see.

Commodores Keyes who, although never having served as a submariner, was appointed Inspecting Captain, 14 November, 1910 and on 31 August, 1912, was appointed to Dolphin as Commodore, Second Class, in charge of the Submarine Service. He was a firm believer in the fleet submarine concept. During 1913 he organised an exercise involving four submarines operating with the fleet behind the forward cruiser screen. The cruisers would inform Keyes, in the destroyer HMS Swift, of the position of the enemy fleet and he would order the submarines to submerge and attack. Because of the submarines slow speed, the exercise was conducted at 14 knots. Despite Keyes admitting to having some very worrying moments as he watched the destroyers and cruisers racing over the positions where the submarines were and the unrealistic speed, he declared the exercise a success.

During August 1914 submarines had been deployed into the Heligoland Bight with surface ships. Three times submarine captains mistakenly identified British ships as the enemy, E6 fired a torpedo at HMS Lowestoft, luckily it just missed. Three British cruises tried to ram British submarines thinking they were U boats. Even after this calamitous episode Keyes was of the opinion that the submarines had shown they could operate with surface ships and they could take care of themselves.

Fisher thought that any fleet that was accompanied by submarines would have a distinct advantage, one of the few things he and Keyes agreed on. Unfortunately, this amenability did not last and two weeks later Fisher dispatched Keyes to the Dardanelles. In his place Fisher appointed Commodore Sydney Hall, who had been in charge of the submarine service between 1906 and 1910, perhaps not surprisingly, Hall was a fleet submarine advocate.

Two months after this, Hall had the unenviable task of telling Fisher that the J Class would not reach the required speed, it could go no faster than 19 knots. The Fleet Flag Officers, Betty and Jellicoe, reemphasised the need for a submarine that could operate with the fleet. They stressed that, with the German's superior diesel technology, the Germans would soon have fleet submarines, in fact they might already have them. This worrying assertion was emphasised when Vickers reported that they could get no more speed from existing diesel engine designs. To overcome these short comings, they proposed a steam driven submarine and forwarded designs for this vessel.

Fisher had no choice but to put aside his reservations about steam power and agree to a steam powered fleet submarine. The d'Eyncourt plans were reviewed and judged against the Vickers design. The d'Eyncourt design was one knot faster and could reach 24 knots, so making it the preferred option. Although it was agreed that the Vickers design had some features that should be included in the final design. The fleet submarine supporters argued that the fleet was being denied valuable and powerful asset. The d'Eyncourt design was a vast improvement on French built Archimede and the method of shutting the funnels and air intakes was robust and dependable.

Fisher suggested that a diesel engine be incorporated in the design, he thought it would provide a degree of redundancy and shorten the time taken to dive or get under way faster when surfacing. An alteration was made to the Boiler Room, in d'Eyncourt's initial design the Boiler Room was shut off when the submarine was on the surface under steam power. This effectively cut the submarine in half, crew couldn't move from fwd to aft. A modification was made and a passageway was installed through the Boiler Room. Further additions to the design were that another gun was added making three and the eight 21 in torpedo were replaced by ten 18 in tubes and two more were fitted in the funnel superstructure.

Fisher ordered four of these submarines and in the beginning of May 1915, d'Eyncourt sent his plans to Vickers. He emphasised that security was of the utmost importance. On 18 June Vickers informed the Admiralty that the submarines would cost £300.000 per boat. This was accepted and a further two boats were ordered from Portsmouth Dockyard. Due to the problematical relationship with Churchill, which came to a head with differences of opinion regarding the Dardanelles campaign, Fisher resigned on 17 May, 1915. After he left office ten more K boats were ordered, three from Vickers, three from Naval Dockyards, two from Armstrong Whitworth and two from the Fairfield yard on the Clyde; these were designated K13 and K14.

Officers such as Admirals Custance and Beresford, who disagreed with Fisher's change agenda, were no more-misguided in looking to the past for direction than Admiral Fisher and his like-minded colleagues were for looking to innovative solutions to solve the problems of the future.

PART 3

K-CLASS SUBMARINES

By any measure, these were impressive, colossal submarines, particularly considering the period in which they were built. They were larger and faster than contemporary destroyers but unfortunately not as maneuverable.

General Characteristics (except K26)

Displacement:	1,980 tons surfaced. 2,566 tons dived
Length:	339 ft (103 m)
Beam:	26 ft 6 in (8.08 m)
Draught:	20 ft 11 in (6.38 m)
Speed:	24 knots (44 km/h) surfaced/8 knots (10 km/h) dived
Propulsion:	Twin 10,500 shp (7.8 MW) oil-fired Yarrow boilers each powering a Brown-Curtis or Parsons geared steam turbines, Twin 3 blade 7 ft 6 in (2.29 m) screws. Four 1,440 hp (1.074 MW) electric motors. One 800 hp (0.6 MW) Vickers diesel generator, for charging batteries on the surface.
Range Surface:	800 nautical miles (1,500 km) at maximum speed, 12,500 miles at 10 knots (20,000 km at 19 km/h)
Range Dived:	8 nautical miles at 8 knots (10 km at 10 km/h), 40 miles at 4 knots (64 km at 7 km/h)
Complement:	59 (6 officers and 53 ratings)

Armament	Four 18 inch (460 mm) beam torpedo tubes, four 18 inch (460 mm) bow tubes, plus 8 spare torpedoes, two 4 inch (100 mm) guns, one 3 inch (80 mm) gun. Twin 18 inch

K3 was the first of the class to be completed in May 1916. Her trials revealed numerous problems, for example, the torpedo swivel tubes were prone to damage and their low freeboard and great length made them awkward to handle, on the surfaced or dived. Their great size combined with their high surface speed, gave them the speed of a destroyer but they had the turning circle of a battle-cruiser, a potentially disastrous combination. The steam power plant required air intakes and funnels. These were large openings in the pressure hull which would be capable of flooding the submarine, if, for some reason, they were not closed correctly. This arrangement lead to the often voiced criticism, that the K class had "too many holes". The submarines had 20 external and 8 internal ballast tanks. To operate the 40 tank vent valves a new hydraulic and telemotor system was developed.

Watertight bulkheads divided the submarine into nine compartments, a watertight hatch allowed access from one compartment to the next. These eight internal bulkheads were designed to withstand a pressure equivalent to only 15 psi, the normal atmospheric pressure.

K Class Submarine Plan

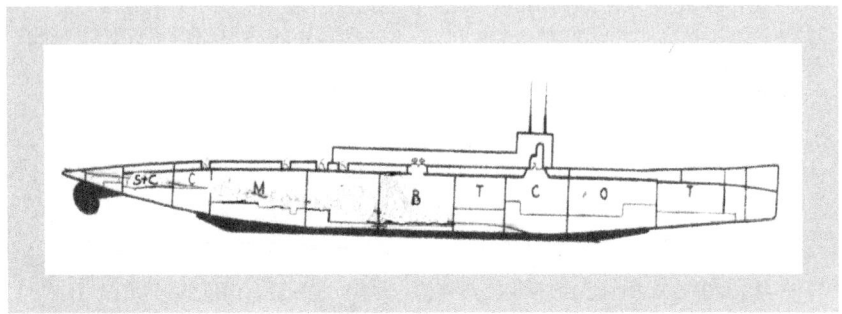

T - Torpedo Room   O – Offices Quarters   C – Control Room B
– Boiler Room   Engine / Turbine Room   M – Machinery
Space   C – Crew Space   S&C   Steering Gear Compartment

The shaded compartments are the ones that were flooded when K13 sank.

The fwd compartment was the Bow Torpedo Room. This contained four 18-inch torpedo tubes, there were 8 reloads. These were 18 inch Mark VIII torpedoes, which were first produced in 1913. They had a range of 2,500 yd (2,300 m) and travelled at 35 knots (65 km/h; 40 mph). The torpedoes were powered by a wet heater which used water to cool the combustion chamber of the fuel-burning torpedo. The torpedoes had a 320 lb (150 kg) TNT warhead and some of the crew ate in this compartment.

Next are the Officers' Quarters. This was a large, relatively luxurious and well-appointed compartment. There were cooking facilities, an oven, hot plate and an urn. There was even a small bath. The Captain had his own cabin. The Battery tank was under the wardroom. There was a hatch, the Fore Hatch, to the casing.

Immediately aft of the Officers' Quarters was the Control Room. This housed the vessel's two periscopes, the Wireless Office, the main switchboard, the gyro compass and the control wheels for the hydroplanes and rudder. Three of the submarine's four toilets were in the Control Room. There was a ladder leading into the

Conning Tower which gave access to the Wheelhouse. The controls to release the fwd of the two 10-ton drop keels were in this compartment.

Between the Control Room and the Boiler Room was the Amidships Torpedo Room. This compartment had a hatch. There were 4 18 inch torpedo tubes, 2 discharging to the starboard side and 2 to the port. There were several reloads.

The Boiler Room housed two 10,500 shp (7.8 MW) oil-fired Yarrow boilers. They provided the steam that powered the Brown-Curtis or Parsons turbines which in turn powered the submarine on the surface at a working pressure of 235lb/in². These gave rise to the submarine's most distinctive feature, its two funnels. These were five-foot high and jutted out from the superstructure, aft of the conning tower. When the submarine dived they were tilted downward by electric motors and housed in the superstructure. This arrangement nullified one of the submarines biggest advantages, stealth. Even on the surface submarines were difficult to see, but with two funnels belching smoke?

On the starboard side of the Boiler-Room there was a watertight passage connecting the Turbine Room and the amidships Torpedo Compartment. At each end of this passage was a watertight door and mid-way a bull's eye looking into the Boiler Room. This passageway, essentially, allowed the crew to move between the two halves of the submarine while steaming on the surface.

There was an air lock between the Boiler Room and Turbine Room. The boilers were "open front" which meant that the Boiler Room had to be pressurised in order to get the air into the furnace.

Air for the boilers entered the Boiler Room through four openings in the pressure hull, 37" in diameter, there were two turbo-fans directly below the intakes to draw air in the compartment. When dived these intakes were covered by metal plates which prevented the seawater from flooding the Boiler Room. The covers were dome-shaped with lugs on the rim, which slid on vertical bars. To open, covers were raised about 10 inch by a hydraulic ram to allow air to enter. Each cover weighed about 8 cwts and this weight helped them close. Several systems were installed to operate the covers. In some designs a hydraulic ram pressed down on the cover to keep it on its seating when shut. On K13 the intakes were kept open by hydraulic pressure on the rams. When the pressure was removed, a spring forced the intake onto its. The covers could also be operated by hand in the event of a hydraulic failure.

The Turbine Room had two hatches to the casing. On the surface power was provided by two sets of geared steam turbines which together developed 10,500 shp, each set consisting of one hp and one LP turbine with an astern turbine incorporated in each LP turbine. Double helical reduction gearing gave shaft revs of 400 rev/min corresponding to turbine speed of hp 3,500 and LP 2,800. The turbines in the Vickers boats were of the Parsons type and in the others of Brown Curtis type. These gave the submarine a surface speed in excess of 21 knots. They also charged the batteries. The control gear for operating the funnels and air intakes was fitted in the turbine room. The intake control valve was fwd on the Boiler Rm / Turbine Rn bulkhead. Electrical indicators were fitted in the Turbine Room to show the position of the air intake covers. When they were shut word was passed to the Commanding Officer in the Control Room via telephone or voice pipe.
The submarines fourth toilet was in the Turbine Room.

Motor Room with Hatch

The submarines were fitted with four 1,440 hp (1.074 MW) electric motors to drive the two shafts while submerged. These gave the vessels an underwater speed of nine knots and a submerged endurance of approximately 80 nautical miles at two knots.

Admiral Fisher had also insisted on an auxiliary diesel engine. This was an E Class eight cylinder 800 bhp diesel and it powered a 700hp dynamo. This provided power on surfacing while steam power was raised. This could produce a surface speed of 9-10 knots. This also provided propulsion just before diving when the boilers were shut down. The diesel was used to charge the batteries.

Crew Space with Hatch

Most of the crew were accommodated here. There was an oven, hot plate and an urn. The crew had to hot bunk, that is two or even three men sharing one bunk, not at the same time.

Steering Compartment

The hydraulic rams for controlling the rudder were in this compartment. This compartment provided more messing space.

Despite their size there was very little space available, there were pipes and valves everywhere and lockers and drawers were crammed in all over the place.

Casing

The K-class submarines were fitted with a proper deckhouse, built over and around the conning tower, which gave the watch keepers much better protection than the canvas screens fitted in earlier Royal Navy submarines. This also provided support for the two wireless masts. A pair of torpedo tubes were fitted in a swivel mounting in the casing. These were intended for night use but were later removed as they were liable to damage in rough seas. There were two four-inch deck guns and a three-inch gun mounted on the casting. There was also a bucket flush toilet in the casing.

There was a coal fired galley in the casing just aft the funnels. To provide fuel for the galley and coal bunker, two tons of coal was taken on board as required, and this is where the joke came from about coaling ship. This also lead to rumours about the submarines being coal powered. As the casing was free flooding, the galley could only be used while the boat was on the surface and the sea moderately calm. However, it did come in very handy while in harbour and it provided a change from the limited cooking facilities offered by hot plates and electric ovens inside the boat.

A small dinghy was also stored in casing.

K-Class submarine showing the original bows

Submarine with the swan bows

K13 was salvaged and recommissioned as K22. She was badly damaged in an incident known as the Battle of May Island on 31 January, 1918.

Habitability – Living Conditions

Despite their enormous size, habitability aboard the K-class submarines was comparatively poor. Although the officers had fairly spacious accommodation, the Captain had his own small cabin and each officer had his own bunk. The wardroom itself was spacious and well furnished, they even had a small four-foot bath with hot water, the water being heated by steam or electricity.

Most of the crew were accommodated in the stern of the submarine and these quarters were cramped and poorly ventilated. Residual heat from the boilers kept the ambient temperature onboard uncomfortably high and the humidity was oppressive. In an attempt to alleviate this problem larger fans were installed in the Boiler Room. The Senior Rates and Engine Room Artificers had separate messes which were separated by a curtain. Living problems were made worse in the crews bunk spaces, each bunk was shared by two, sometimes three, men. There was little in the way of privacy. Also, the self-compensating fuel tanks formed the deck of these crew's spaces and during a dive the oil was often forced through the seams and coated the decks. The Admiralty exacerbated these problems by insisting that the submarines were self-contained, independent commands and as such the crew had to live aboard, even when alongside in port.

The submarine's crew were divided into three watches, Red, White and Blue. When at sea, apart from when the submarine was at Action Stations, one third of the crew were on watch, actual manning / driving the submarine. The rest of the crew either rested or performed various maintenance tasks, domestic duties such as cooking or cleaning. Each watch lasted four hours during the day and three hours at night. This put a great deal of pressure on the crew. Also, the limited number of personnel on board increased the individual workload. No chefs, stewards etc. were carried, so these additional duties had to be shared out amongst those available.

To avoid detection, submarines were often dived during the day, they would then surface at night to run diesels and recharge their batteries. The crew took the opportunity to cook a hot meal. The on-board ovens were not particularly efficient and could not be used when the submarine was dived because of the load they imposed on the battery. The heat they generated made the already humid atmosphere even worse.

The galley in the casing enabled all the messes to prepare their food at the same time. There were two or three reports which might have suffered a certain amount of submariner elaboration. Where the First Lieutenant had written in the Night Order Book, "As there will be no diving tomorrow, the upper deck galley can be used." In this case, the duty quartermaster of the morning watch would light the galley range, collect all the messes roasts, fannies of peas and greens and nets of potatoes, and on leaving harbour, if not having another duty to perform, would arm himself with a book, go into the galley in the casing, find a box to sit on and sit down and enjoy a read and supervise the cooking of all the messes dinners. Occasionally there would be a change of programme, only known to the Captain, and the submarine would be dived to carry for some reason. As a result, the galley was flooded as the boat submerged and the dinners were lost. The duty chef had to race out of the galley and try to get into the wheelhouse before they closed the top hatch leading to the Control Room.

The stowage of food was certainly an afterthought if a thought at all. Space had to be found that would have a minimal effect on the submarines operational effectiveness. Not the easiest of tasks considering the cramped onboard conditions. Stowages had to be found where the food wouldn't come adrift in rough weather and it had to be evenly spread throughout the submarine to have the minimal effect on the trim. Access had to be available to allow the crew to see gauges and operate valves. Fridges were not allowed on board as the coolant gasses were considered a health risk. This and the damp environment made the keeping of fresh food difficult. This obviously had an unhealthy impact on the crew's diet. Fresh water supplies were very limited. This restricted the options available to the chefs and added to this, the water was often tainted by fuel.

The navy did not supply all the food used on board. Things that were considered as non-essential had to be bought by the crew with an allowance known as Canteen Messing. Things such as milk, tea and coffee had to be purchased. The wardroom organised their own food supplies.

Obviously, tinned food was supplied. Tinned meat was introduced into the Navy in 1853. The introduction was slow and until the early years of the war, large stocks of salted meat were held. A common meal was Hard Tack Hash, which was a mixture of crumbled ships biscuits and tinned corned beef. The urns could be used at all times and the crew sustained themselves between often infrequent meals with hot drinks, a particular favorite being hot coca.

Leisure facilities were practically non-existent. There simply wasn't the space, only packs of cards, books and magazines were available. Some boats had gramophones. The lack of exercise had a detrimental effect on the crew's general health, constipation being one of the main complications. The crew's onboard living and working conditions were smelly, damp, often hot, very uncomfortably, there was a lack of privacy and they were extremely cramped. These unpleasant conditions were somewhat offset by the traditional daily rum ration. The crew could also smoke.

Handling Characteristics

Once under way, on the surface, the boats lacked buoyance forward and tended to plough into oncoming waves, shipping tons of water over the conning tower and casing, several submarines had their bridge windows broken. In these conditions the Captains had no choice but to either reduce speed or dive. The forward gun could not be manned as it always was half submerged and the deck torpedo tubes could not be used. They were also prone to damage in rough seas and were later removed. Water coming down the conning tower would short out the electrics and made parts of the ladder electrically live. The large, flat foredeck tended to force the bow down. To counter this the entire class was later fitted with a bulbous, free-flooding prow known as a "swan bow". Despite this modification they rarely could operate with the Battle Fleet in the North Sea at the required speed, except in the most benign weather conditions. The submarines were susceptible to being pooped by following seas. Sea water entering the Boiler Room through the funnels extinguished the fires and left the submarine powerless. Especially in rough weather, the fuel in the self-compensating tanks, which were open to the sea from below, could mix with the seawater. This extinguished the fires in the boilers.

If the submarine's performance on the surface gave cause for concern, dived, it was disturbing in the extreme. It took the submarines normally 30 minutes to dive. This was the minimum time required to secure the main engines and shift to battery motors. The boiler fires had to be extinguished, a complicated series of hydraulics and mechanical rods and levers lowered the twin funnels into wells in the superstructure, as well as simultaneously closing hatches over the funnel uptakes. The main air intakes were closed along with sea water connections for condensers and boiler feed. During this period, the Boiler Room was uninhabitable due to the high residual heat. K8 once succeeded in submerging in 3 minutes, 25 seconds, but trying to complete the complicated series of actions required before the submarine could dive quickly could invite mistakes. Many Captains took advantage of this extended dive time to walk around the casing and ensure the funnels and intakes were securely closed.

The traditional "Crash" dive, which could be considered to have been almost a tactical weapon on current submarines, was certainly not part of the K-class repertoire. It was considered that with their speed of 24 knots (44 km/h; 28 mph), there was no need for the ability to crash dive. If the submarines were attacked on the surface, their speed would enable them to turn and simply outrun almost any threat.

The flat areas of the superstructure acted as hydroplanes, and once the submarine started to dive, they were hard to stop. Loss of depth control was common and nosing into the bottom was a regular occurrence, particularly as efficient telemotor controls had not yet been developed. Unless the submarine was very carefully trimmed, the hydroplanes and ballast tanks would frequently fail to correct her, particularly since the hydroplanes sometimes jammed. A 10-degree angle, bow down angle, would cause a 59-foot (18 m) difference in depth between the bow and stern, a 30 degree angle, would produce a 170 foot (52 m) difference. This would put the stern, practically, on the surface, while the bow would be below the maximum design diving depth of 150 feet. Fortunately, the K-boats operated mostly in the North Sea where the water was shallow enough to keep them from exceeding their depth limits in the dive. Their erratic behavior did not bode well for operating with surface ships.

Their large size made them difficult to handle and lack of experience among commanding officers and their crews in handling submarines of this size, exacerbated this. These problems were further compounded by the fact that the submarine was, essentially, in two halves. Aft tanks were flooded and blow from aft, for'd tanks were controlled from the Control Room. This arrangement made trimming and ballasting the vessel a nightmare.

A similar arrangement was used for the two drop keels. Initially the Admiralty didn't fit drop keels to submarines. These had been used from the earliest times to give submarines extra buoyancy in case of an emergency. The Admiralty was of the opinion that any accident that was sudden enough to sink the submarine would be too devastating for a drop keel to be of any use. This view was only changed after the detachable keel of the French Bonire saved her crew after a collision in February 1906.

No	Builder	Commissioned	Fate
K1	Portsmouth Dockyard	May 1917	sunk after collision with K4, November 17, 1917
K2	Portsmouth Dockyard	February 1917	scrapped 1926
K3	Vickers (Barrow-in-Furness)	August 1916	scrapped 1920
K4	Vickers	January 1917	sunk after collision with K6, 31 January, 1918
K5	Portsmouth Dockyard	May 1917	lost on exercises, 20 January, 1921
K6	Devonport Dockyard	June 1917	scrapped 1926
K7	Devonport Dockyard	July 1917	scrapped 1919
K8	Vickers	March 1917	scrapped 1923
K9	Vickers	May 1917	scrapped 1921
K10	Vickers	June 1917	scrapped 1921
K11	Armstrong Whitworth	February 1917	scrapped 1921

(Tyneside)

K12	Armstrong Whitworth	August 1917	scrapped 1926
K13	Fairfield's (Clydeside)	-	sank on acceptance trials, 29 January, 1917. Raised and renumbered K22
K14	Fairfield's (Clydeside)	May 1917	scrapped 1925
K15	Scott's (Clydeside)	May 1918	sank in Portsmouth Harbour, 25 June 1921; raised and scrapped, 1923
K16	Beardmore's (Clydeside)	May 1918	scrapped 1923
K17	Vickers	March 1917	sunk after collision with HMS Fearless, 31 January 1918
K18	Vickers	April 1918	became submarine monitor M1; sunk after collision with SS Vidar, 12 November, 1925
K19	Vickers	November 1919	became submarine monitor M-2; sank on exercises, 26 January, 1932

K20	Armstrong Whitworth	1920	became submarine monitor M-3; scrapped 1932
K21	Armstrong Whitworth	-	laid down as submarine monitor M-4; cancelled
K22 (x K13)	raised and refitted by Fairfield's	October 1917	scrapped 1926
K23	Armstrong Whitworth	-	cancelled
K24	Armstrong Whitworth	-	cancelled
K25	Armstrong Whitworth	-	cancelled
K26	Vickers and Chatham Dockyard	May 1923	scrapped 1931
K27	Vickers	-	cancelled
K28	Vickers	-	cancelled

Despite this, the K-class could indeed make 24 knots on the surface, when the seas weren't too rough, and this record was not exceeded by any other submarine, until the arrival of the nuclear powered craft.

K26, the last and improved boat, was completed slowly, finally being commissioned in 1923. She had six 21-inch (530 mm) bow torpedo tubes but retained the 18-inch beam tubes. Her higher casing almost cured the problems of seawater entering the boiler room and improved ballast tank arrangements. The diving time to just over 3 minutes to dive to 80 feet (24 m). She also had an increased maximum diving depth of 250 feet (76 m).

The submarines developed an unenviable safety record, they were involved in numerous accidents, largely as a result of their poor maneuverability. Six boats sank and they were involved in sixteen major accidents.

K1 had so many sea trials, during speed runs, her Boiler and Turbine Rooms became so hot that the hatches had to be left open, and a head sea cracked the conning tower windows. During one of her early test dives she uncontrollably dived and burrowed her bow into the muddy sea-bed while her propellers were above the surface. It took 20 minutes to get her back to the surface. Unfortunately, the future King George VI, Prince George, was onboard as an observer. In January 1917, on one of her first war patrols from the Grand Fleet's main operating base at Scapa Flow in the Orkney Islands, she took so much water down the funnels, that her Boiler Room flooded. Luckily Admiral Fisher's auxiliary diesel engine managed to get her back to port. She also held the unofficial record for maximum diving depth (266 feet), after an uncontrolled dive to the bottom of the Pentland Firth.

K4 ran aground at Walney Island, in January 1917.

K5 was lost during an exercise in the Bay of Biscay on 20 January 1921. Nothing further was heard of her following a signal that she was diving, but wreckage was recovered later that day. It was concluded that she exceeded her safe maximum depth.

K6 wouldn't surface after a trial dive in a basin in Devonport Dockyard.

On 29th January 1917, K13 dived in the Gare Loch as part of her acceptance trials, the Boiler Room flooded and the sub sank to the bottom of the loch in 65 ft of water. She was salvaged and recommissioned as K22.

During her trials, K14, flooded the battery tank under the Officers' Quarters, after the plates over B ballast tank had worded loose. There were also several electrical fires.

Two boats were lost in an incident that became known as the Battle of May Island on 31 January 1918. The cruiser HMS Fearless collided with the head of a line of submarines, K17, which sank in about 8 minutes, whilst other submarines behind her all turned to avoid her. K4 was struck by K6 which almost cut her in half and was then struck by K7 before she finally sank with all her crew. At the same time K22 and K14 collided although both survived. In just 75 minutes, two submarines had been sunk, three badly damaged and 105 crew killed.

In May 1921, K15 shipped water down her funnels, this doused the furnace fires and caused her to sink to the bottom, stern first. Luckily, quick action by the Captain and crew prevented loss of life. On 25 June 1921, she sank at her mooring in Portsmouth. In the hot weather the hydraulic oil expanded, then contracted overnight as the temperature dropped. The consequent loss of pressure caused the ballast tank vents to open. As the submarine submerged, she flooded through open hatches.

K16 and K12 also sank in the Gareloch; their crews were luckier than the crew of K13, in that after several hours submerged they managed to surface.

In June 1917, four K-class submarines were on an anti-submarine sweep in the North Sea accompanied by destroyers and other submarines. During the ten day operation no U-boats were sunk, but the Germans managed to sink nine British merchant ships that were under the protection of the British force. Unfortunately, one of the K-class submarines (K7) was mistakenly identified as a German U-boat and depth charged by two British destroyers. Luckily the attack was unsuccessful. K7 then located a U-boat and fired a torpedo at it, at point blank range, it hit the target but failed to explode. The Fair Isle lighthouse reported K2 lost with all hands. The keepers believed she had hit a mine after they saw an explosion. The Admiralty sent out telegrams informing the next of kin of the loss, understandably the families were shattered. However, two days later an unidentified submarine entered Scarpa Flow at night and luckily, in the ensuing panic, no one fired on her. It was K2, the explosion the lighthouse keepers had seen was the submarine firing its gun at the lighthouse!

Apart from these troubles, there were design flaws with all the K-Class and there were numerous smaller defects. These included gas leaks, explosions, boiler fires and hydraulic failures.

Several of the submarines suffered fwd hydroplanes jam when the submarine went below 80 ft while others had trouble with the aft hydroplanes. It was thought that the control gear might not have been strong enough or that the stern may have compressed and distorted under pressure, jamming the bearings in the control gear.

Despite all this, K-class submarines were still being constructed after the war and still getting into trouble. On 25th June 1921, K15 sunk at its mooring at Portsmouth. It was due to a loss of hydraulic pressure causing dive vents to open. Also in this year, K22 dived with both her funnels up.
Most were scrapped between 1921 and 1926 but K26 survived until 1931, then being broken up because her displacement exceeded the limits for submarine displacement in the London Naval Treaty of 1930. K18, K19 and K20 became the new M-class submarines. K21, K23, K24, K25, K27 and K28 were cancelled. Although the concept of a submarine fast enough to operate with a battle fleet eventually fell out of favour, it was still an important consideration in the design of the River class in the late 1920s.

Discussion

It does not seem unreasonable to ask why the Admiralty would continue to operate these submarines, particularly when there was more than enough information to hand detailing the handling problems and the faults that plagued the submarines.

Of the thirteen submarines that carried out trials between January and May 1917, all of them had problems. Over the years the class was in service, six boats sank, there were sixteen major accidents and, unfortunately, over three hundred service and civilian personnel lost their lives serving in or working on these submarines, not one of them as a result of enemy action.

The rationale behind this decision is understandable; the Admiralty viewed warfare in terms of big fleet actions, rows of battleships, essentially, slogging it out. This was only 100 years after Trafalgar, and although the hardware had changed beyond all recognition, the basic underlying policy was the same. This was the way the Navy thought that battles would be decided, by massed fleets fighting one another. Everything had to support this philosophy and, in the days when airplane reconnaissance was non-existent, was the idea of a submarine, capable of high surface speeds, operating with the fleet such an irrational one? It is very easy, with a hundred years of hindsight, to challenge the Admiralty's rational, but everything had to reinforce this philosophy. The Navy was certainly defensive about the submarines, maybe even in denial. Reputations were at risk, the building dockyards, high ranking naval officers and civil servants all had interest in seeing the submarines succeed. Also, if these incidents were made public, it was thought it might have a detrimental effect on crew's moral.

No one seems to have viewed the incidents in the whole, they appear to have been analysed separately, and, perhaps not surprisingly, they reached the conclusion that the various incidents were the teething problems that were to be expected with any newly designed, complex vessel. They thought the solution would be to simply inform the submarine's Commanding Officers how to deal with them or preferably how to avoid them all together.

Rear-Admiral Ernest Leir, a very experienced submariner who had had several commands including a K boat, commented, "The only good thing about K boats was that they never engaged the enemy." The debate about the efficacy of the K-class submarines rages on. Some 50 years later, in response to Don Everitt's book, K Boats, a reviewer, writing in the Naval Review, wrote a very robust defence of the Navy's position. While conceding the fact that Mr. Everitt's researches were very thorough, and no one could quarrel with the facts as presented in the book, the reviewer felt that the book over dramatised the history of the K-class of submarine. The reviewer, Eeyore Smith, actually served on K-class submarines and disagrees with the conclusions Everitt reaches in his book. He recalls the First Submarine Flotilla under Captains Horton and Talbot as hard-working and happy and the attitude of the crews who manned the vessels hardly matches Mr. Everitt's contention that 'they became the objects of much superstition, hatred and contention'. The K-class veterans even had their own association, the Brighter K-boat Society, which meets on numerous festive occasions. This doesn't seem to be the action of dispirited, discontented ex crew members trying to forget their harrowing time on these horrific vessels. The Reviewer contends that the boats were OK and most of the incidents could be put down to human error. Although he concedes that they were too narrow for their length, their pressure hulls far too weak and their main-ballast blowing system was too feeble for the job.

But were the K-class submarines really that bad? Did they deserve such epithets as K for Kalamity, K for kasastrophe, K for koffin? I've even seen K for killer. I can't help but feel these were added by latter day writers in an attempt to spice up their accounts. Was the term Suicide Club really coined by the crews to describe their destiny, did they really believe this?
Even among the submariner cadre there is always somebody who will complain, but did these expressions represent the feelings and concerns of the whole flotilla? Was Mr. Smith the only K boat crew member who thought they were any good?

What is undeniable is that the submarines certainly had an abysmal safety record. There was a vast catalogue of accidents and incidents due to design and system faults and it must be remembered that there was limited experience in handling such large subs and their new control systems. These were compounded by the operational policy; surface maneuvering in close company with surface units was never the strong suit of submarine captains, they were individualists. The Fleet boat concept required them to be experts in surface maneuvering, similar to their counterparts in destroyers.

The submarines certainly met the required specification regarding speed. Unfortunately, the only way this could be achieved was by using steam turbines and this came with the attendant problems of funnels air intakes, too many damned holes.

The crews were generally not to blame for the plethora of accidents that befell their vessels, in fact, several of the boats were saved by the actions of their crews. For example, K12 and K16 both sank in the Gare Loch but thanks to the efforts of their crews, both were able to surface safely. They made the best of a bad job, generally just got on with the job, hampered by being shackled to the wrong policy, the lack of experience with the new technology and perhaps admiralty pride. They were a concept before their time and despite this, the crews did an effective, good job and Mr Smith felt that by the early twenties, the K-class and their crews had reached a high degree of efficiency, much the same as you would find on any other class of submarine.

PART 4

THE CREWS

Regardless of the concerns expressed by the naval traditionalists and their supporters, by 1914 the Submarine Service was an integral part of the Royal Navy and the worries expressed by these early critics had largely been addressed. That aside, there was still a lack of understanding about the capabilities of the submarine, or how they could be used in combat and what role they would play during periods of hostilities. As they became more reliable and effective there was a growing awareness of their prospective abilities. This was enhanced by the growing acceptance of these new craft within the general naval community. The ability and confidence being shown by the submarine's commanding officers and their crews further amplified this view.

But who were these men who manned these craft and put up with the discomfort and the very real dangers that serving on them entailed? It would be reassuring, even inspiring, to think of them as visionary champions of the new-fangled craft, who had a genuine and strongly held commitment to the future of submarines. After all, submarines were unique, undeniably different, unlike any other type of warship. Certainly, this was part of the attraction for many of the volunteers. Even without the stress and anxieties of war, a submariner's professionalism, technical expertise and resilience was being put to the test from the very moment he boarded his boat.

While the technical complexity of these craft was the main appeal for some, others were attracted by the comradery that was part of being a member of such a small and close-knit ship's company. It was also a welcome break from the traditional navy's, polished brass and regimented routines. They were allowed to be the characters they undoubtedly were and this was a very attractive option for some. These small craft and their scruffy crews were a complete anathema to the smartly uniformed officers and men of the traditional surface Navy, this may have been a valid recruiting point in itself. The responsibility and even the risks were an attraction for some of the volunteers and officers could reach command much earlier than their General Service counterparts.

The truth is probably a little more mundane. While some were undoubtedly enthusiastic supporters of the submarine, who reveled in the comradery and loved the responsibility, for the majority the reasons for volunteering were more self-centered.

Extra pay undoubtedly played a major part in attracting volunteers to 'The Trade', the name young submariners used to describe their chosen profession. Lieutenants and above received six shillings a day extra. If they had command of the submarine, they earned 20s. 9d a day, a very attractive sum of money and more than double a lieutenant's standard pay. An Able Seaman was paid £30 8s 4d per year but if he decided to join the submarine service, he received an extra £36 10s a year. An impressive and undoubtedly welcome increase on his basic pay. Commodore S S Hall, the Captain Inspecting Submarine, thought that the extra pay was reasonable in view of the responsibilities and discomforts experienced by submariners when compared to their surface counterparts. He also felt that without this extra money it would be difficult, if not impossible, to find enough volunteers to man the expanding submarine service.

Submariners also benefited from Blood Money. This was a traditional financial reward given to crews of ships that sank an enemy vessel. Dating from the days of sail, £5 was paid for every enemy serviceman killed or put out of action when his ship was sunk. The smaller ships companies on submarines made for a larger individual payment.

Other than the additional money, submariners benefited from extra shore leave allowance. Many personnel lived in the Portsmouth area, primarily because most submarines were based in HMS Dolphin. As the submarines tended to return to their port each evening, the crews could go home unlike their surface counterparts who could be deployed for months, sometimes, years at a time.
Before 1910, submariners were not liable for service overseas, another reason to join the fledgling service.

Also, submariners were allowed to count service in their craft as sea-time, even if they were drafted to harbour-defence duties. Since a fixed period of sea service was required to qualify for promotion to a higher rank, this was a significant concession.

Because recruiting the necessary manpower was a problem for the service, these privileges were important, particularly as the branch was all-volunteers. The commanders also felt that it wouldn't be right to draft men into such a potentially dangerous occupation. This policy ensured that the branch was not manned by unhappy and uncooperative draftees from General Service. In 1904 the Admiralty made the submarine branch a closed service. Submarine commanding officers couldn't draft men back to General Service and officers and men were required to sign on for five years. After this they would serve at least two years General Service and then, if required, return to submarines for a further three years.

Manpower problems were further compounded by the rapid expansion of the service. By 1913 the closed service arrangement was unable to maintain the manpower requirements. To alleviate this, Keyes proposed that personnel should be allowed to serve in submarines indefinitely; men should be allowed to spend their whole careers in the submarine service. He argued that it was intolerable that highly trained personnel should be lost to the service after a few years' service or were serving their three years with the fleet, stating:

"the efficient manning of this rapidly expanding service is becoming increasingly difficult under the existing regulations."

In the Autumn of 1913, the Admiralty granted Keyes's request. By adopting this policy, the navy enabled submariners to spend more time developing their skills and capabilities. This in turn resulted in the high standards of professionalism that were demonstrated by the British submarine service during the Great War.

But by making the branch a closed service, the Navy risked producing a highly-trained group of out-of-touch specialists, who, in all probability, would be unsuitable for General Service after their spell in submarines. It was also thought that they would probably obstruct advancement rosters across the fleet.

The Navy actively supported the development of close-knit groups. This probably wasn't such a bad thing but submariners positively reveled in their piratical reputation. It bolstered their sense of identity and provided a tenuous justification for their unruly, boisterous and somewhat undisciplined attitude.

Being in this rather unique club allowed them to indulge in their own distinct and often peculiar dress code. This obviously did little to endear them to their smarter and cleaner General Service counterparts who labelled these grubby submarine officers as "unwashed chauffeurs". The following examples will explain why this is an understandable view. One young submarine commanding officer confessed that, after five days at sea, he and his crew looked "a pretty filthy lot of pirates". Even more senior officers were not immune to these unusual dress standards. Lieutenant-Commander H Shove was noted for his "matted, disheveled hair and a high watermark above his collar". It was reported that he kept a pet rat up the sleeve of his monkey jacket. Commander Frank Brandt had an unannounced visit from the Admiral who was in charge of Devonport Dockyard. He arrived on the casing to greet the Admiral, wearing carpet slippers, his trousers were turned up and his pink flannel shirt was visible through his unbuttoned monkey jacket.

Perhaps to help relieve the stresses that were a consequence of their occupation, many of the young submariners rode motorbikes, needless to say rather recklessly. Max Horton was known as "a desperate motorcyclist" and E C Boyle was actually charged with knocking down a teenage girl while riding is motorbike. Even the first submarine VC, Lieutenant Norman Holbrook was said to drive his motorbike rather "furiously".

But before joining this exclusive club, the recruit had to forth fill certain criteria: The Navy could afford to pick the very best after a thorough selection process. Potential submariners had to be effective and efficient workers who were intelligent enough to use machinery that was advanced and complex for this era. They also had to be literate.

There was a strict and comprehensive medical examination before being accepted into the service and they were regularly re-examined. Due to the demanding and arduous nature of service onboard a submarine, there was genuine concern for the health of the crews of these craft. The ratings, who were normally confined below, were thought to be especially at risk, particularly from the engine fumes. Volunteers had to be in good health with no evidence of cardiac or pulmonary disease. They had to be free from rheumatism, syphilis, albuminuria, ear, nose or skin disease, no history of fits or alcohol excess. Volunteers had to exhibit no signs of hernia, varicose veins, arterial degeneration or oral sepsis. Anyone who was or had suffered from any of these was immediately rejected. It was essential that crew members were healthy, both physically and mentally.

The lack of fresh air and the restricted space on these early submarines made it essential to keep crew numbers to a minimum. As a consequence of this, if a crew member became ill at sea, his duties would have to be covered by other crew members. There were little or no facilities to treat an ill crew member on board and this affected both the operational efficiency and the moral of the crew. The cramped living conditions meant that any potentially communicative disease could seriously impact the operational effectiveness of the submarine. The lack of washing facilities made crew members particularly prone to skin conditions, especially as they were in contact with many irritants.

Those volunteers who made it past the selection process and medical examination then faced a lengthy training programme. It is little wonder that those who joined the Submarine Service saw themselves as an elite force. This opinion was further endorsed by the fact that it was the stated opinion of several Inspecting Captains of Submarines, that the safe operation of the submarines depended upon minimising the possibility of human error. This required crews that were not only highly skilled but also highly trained. The necessary high standards were achieved by only accepting volunteers who were rated as 'above average' during their initial training and following this with a period of intense training. These recruits were slowly introduced into the service so as not to dilute the existing experienced crews with too many new. As policy, the Submarine Service tried to keep experienced crews together and accept only enough volunteers to replace natural wastage plus a margin to allow for expansion.

It is not clear-cut to when formalised Submarine Training began, for either Officers and Ratings. In the early days training appears to have been made up as it went along. Initial training procedures for the Holland Class seem to have been a combined effort by 'Captain' Cable (from Electric Boat) and Captain Bacon, the first Inspecting Captain of Submarines. After that it appears that Submarine experience was passed on from qualified Officers and Senior Ratings on an 'ad hoc' basis.

Initially training was carried out in the submarine depot ship at various ports around the country but gradually it was centralised at HMS Dolphin. The beginnings of the school appear to go back to 1905, when rudimentary submarine training started in a group of three huts at Fort Blockhouse. New recruits underwent a three months' training, largely theoretical, often using decommissioned submarines that were laid up in the harbour. The instructors were experienced Senior Rates from the Submarine Service. Some training seems to have been conducted at sea, as on 8th May 1905 A8 sank off Plymouth with a training class of one officer and seven ratings on board, unfortunately the whole class was lost in the accident.

A more novel training method was adopted on certain

building submarines. There is a report of a boat's First Lieutenant who commandeered a disused shed in the shipyard's premises. Using chalk, he marked the submarine's most important valves and wheels on the walls and floor and instructed the crew on various drills before the submarine left the yard. Though the men were amused at this novel training method, they undoubtedly learnt a great good deal about the various routines they would use once they were at sea.

In peace time an officer who wished to join the Submarine Service had to be recommended by his Commanding Officer. He required a first-class certificate from his Torpedo examination for Lieutenant, or a certificate from the Torpedo-Lieutenant of his ship saying he had an aptitude for that particular aspect of his duties. If accepted he was eventually appointed to Fort Blockhouse, where he would join the new officers class and undergo the rigorous medical examination. Then there was a three-month period of practical submarine instruction, this terminated in several examinations. Failure in any of them resulted in him being returned to General Service.

On successful completion of his course he would be sent as "third hand" to a submarine until a vacancy occurred as a First Lieutenant. After several years in this position he would be appointed in command of an A boat. As he gained command experience and seniority, he would be appointed to larger submarines. Since 1917 all potential Executive Officers were required to take the 24 week long 'Perisher' which is the informal name given to the Royal Navy's Submarine Command Course. Two courses are run each year, normally starting 2 July and 14 November. One in four of the personnel attending the course fail, it is widely regarded as one of the toughest command courses in the world.

Ratings underwent a process similar to that of officers to

gain entry to the service. They had to be recommended, be of first-class character and of course pass the stringent medical exam. The training was similar but not as comprehensive as the officers. Failure on any part of the course resulted in the rating being returned to General Service.

And once he had passed the rigorous medical examination and completed his training, what was the newly qualified submariner entitled to? Essentially it allowed him to live in a cramped, narrow, constantly damp, smelly steel tube under the sea. The amount of condensation made it impossible to keep clothes dry and when the submarine was on the surface, sea water often cascaded through hatches. The submarine's atmosphere was often stale, even in calm seas, and even with the hatches open, few of the crew got much in the way of fresh air. The air that was available was polluted by petrol or diesel fumes, stank of food, sweat and frequently of vomit; in the early boats the toilets were little more than pails, these arrangements did little to improve the situation. The boat was unpleasantly hot in summer and decidedly cold in winter or when it was under water.

The conditions on the early submarines were so bad that Admiral Fisher opined, "the only limit to their marvelous efficiency is the endurance of the crews". These words must have delighted the submarine crews because based on this it can be assumed that crew endurance had been considerably under-estimated. Before 1914 it was widely believed that crew stamina rather than mechanical or logistical limitations would dictate the time a submarine could spend at sea. To overcome this, it was suggested that each submarine should have two crews but due to the manning demands of the rapidly expanding service this was unworkable. An alternative was to provide 'spare crews' who would take over the submarine when it returned to port and carry out routine tasks, battery charging etc. so the 'operational' crew could be released for the evening.

These unhealthy and potentially precarious conditions were partly offset by the crews being billeted in the slightly more spacious surroundings of depot ships when not at sea in their submarines. Undoubtedly, the daily rum ration, or "tot", helped the crews cope with the conditions. It consisted of one-eighth of an imperial pint (71 ml) of rum that was 95.5 proof. It was issued at midday to the crew, officers excluded. In 1970, Admiral Peter Hill-Norton, finally, abolished the rum ration on 31st July 1970, this became known as Black Tot Day. The crews could also smoke, on the surface there was generally no restrictions, unless the battery was being charged. Once dived smoking was not allowed, that was unless the Captain was a smoker in which case, a regular 'one all-round' was the order of the day.

As mentioned earlier in this chapter, habitability standards and recreational opportunities aboard submarines were practically non-existent, even on the larger submarines such as the K-Class. Despite this, or maybe because of this, British submariners were well trained, professional, committed and generally happy with their lot. By 1914 British submariners were unquestionably more uniformly competent than those of any other nation.

During the war, Rudyard Kipling wrote a booklet he called The Fringes of the Fleet, a series of essays and poems on various nautical aspects of the war. Some of the poems were set to music by English composer Edward Elgar.

They bear, in place of classic names,
Letters and numbers on their skin.
They play their grisly blindfold games
In little boxes made of tin.
Sometimes they stalk the Zeppelin,
Sometimes they learn where mines are laid,
Or where the Baltic ice is thin.
That is the custom of "The Trade."

Few prize-courts sit upon their claims.
They seldom tow their targets in.
They follow certain secret aims
Down under, far from strife or din.
When they are ready to begin
No flag is flown, no fuss is made
More than the shearing of a pin.
That is the custom of "The Trade."

The Scout's quadruple funnel flames
A mark from Sweden to the Swin,
The Cruiser's thund'rous screw proclaims
Her comings out and goings in:
But only whiffs of paraffin
Or creamy rings that fizz and fade
Show where the one-eyed Death has been.
That is the custom of "The Trade."

Their fears, their fortunes and their fames
Are hidden from their nearest kin;
No eager public backs or blames,
No journal prints the yarn they spin
(The Censor would not let it in!)

When they return from run or raid.
Unheard they work, unseen they win.
That is the custom of "The Trade."

CHAPTER 2

THE ACCIDENT

Three years after the sinking of K13, in 1920, AB Sidney Glazebrook, a 20 yr. old gunner, met his friend, Leading Telegraphist Charles Freestone, a K13 survivor, in the Kepples Head Hotel on Portsmouth Hard. They were having a farewell drink before Charles sailed to Australia on submarine J2. They were unexpectedly joined by Lt Cdr Herbert, the K13's commanding officer and naturally the conversion turned to K13 and the events of 29 January 1917. They discussed the possibility of visiting Govan, on the anniversary of the accident, to lay a wreath.

PART 1

THE ACCIDENT

The Admiralty ordered two submarines from Fairfield Shipbuilders at Govan. The contract was signed 6 August 1915, and the submarines were given the Job No's 522 and 523, they were designated K13 and K14. The contract stated that the boats would be completed within 12 months, but K13 took nearer to 14 months. Although the K-class design was well established with several submarines under construction at other yards, Fairfield had to incorporate all the modifications agreed and changes required to suit sub-contractors' equipment that was used on other submarines being built.

The keel of K13 was laid down 2 October 1916 and she was launched at 13:45 11 November 1916 by Mrs Herbert, the wife of the submarine's Commanding Officer, Lt Cdr Godfrey Herbert. Unfortunately, the hydroplanes were damaged as the submarine ran down the slipway.

After this was repaired, the submarine was carrying out a static basin dive where she slowly submerged, allowing ship's staff to calculate the trim and check for leaks. The submarine unexpectedly sank to the bottom. Luckily the basin wasn't very deep so the submarine was not totally submerged. Not so lucky were an Admiralty Overseer and a Fairfield Director who were on the casing at the time and finished up getting thoroughly soaked.

Once completed, the submarine was moved to Govan Dry Dock for final painting. While she was in the dock the gates were opened to allow another vessel in. Regrettably casing valves in the engine room had been left open which resulted in the engine and motor room being flooded.

She carried out preliminary trials on 29 of December 1916, official speed trials on 18 January1917. During the speed trials, she covered the measured mile at a record 23 knots and gained the honour of being the world's fastest submarine. She damaged her funnels in heavy seas. It was reported that only the determined bailing out of the engine room prevented the ship from filling with water and sinking. This was followed by dives at Fairfield on 6 and 7 January. On Saturday 20 January, she carried out a successful dive to a depth of 65 feet in the Gare Loch and remained submerged for about an hour.

She was due to leave the yard for her final acceptance trials at 0800 Monday 29 January 1917 but a problem with one of the mooring wires caused a delay. On board were 80 men; 53 RN crew, 14 employees of the Govan ship builder, 5 Admiralty officials, 5 other civilians, a pilot and the captain and engineer of sister submarine K14, which was also building at Fairfield, to gain K-boat experience. She had only travelled a mile down the river when the steering motor was accidentally switched off. This caused the submarine to ground at Whiteinch, with her bows on a mud bank, where the ebbing tide caused her stern to swing across the river. This lead to a heated exchange with the Captain of the SS Sunniva, who tried to steer his ship through the rapidly narrowing gap between the stern of the submarine and the opposite river bank. Lt Cdr Herbert, K13's Commanding Officer, allowed the tide to bring the stern right around before going astern on the engines and proceeding, somewhat incongruously, backwards down the Clyde. It was only when he reached a tributary, known as the Cart, that he had room to put her about.

January the 29th was the day selected for us to leave the Fairfield Yard to do our acceptance trials, and it proved a fatal one. We started very badly for just after leaving the Yard, our steering gear gave out and we ran high and dry on the banks of the Clyde. We soon had two powerful tugs alongside us, and with their assistance, we managed to get off although we had to be towed stern first until we got to a wider spot where it was possible to turn round. We now continued our journey down the Clyde and at 10.0 am we entered the "Gareloch".
Cox'n Oscar Moth

In Cox'n Moth's recollection of the day he states that the submarine was 'pulled' off the mud bank by two powerful tugs. Another account states that the grounding was caused by a towing hawser from one of the tugs parting.

K13 reached the Gare Loch by 11:30; she carried out full power trials and other tests that were required as part of the acceptance programme; starting, stopping, full speed, turning, going astern. All of these were completed successfully. During the trial dive, her depth was gradually increased to 83 feet, she remained submerged for approximately 2 hours. When she resurfaced her Engineer, Lieutenant Arthur Lane, reported that there was a small leak in the boiler room and that some 200 gallons of water had entered the compartment. The heat in the boiler room made it impossible for anyone to determine the source of the leak. He suggested a further short dive to determine the source of the leak and to check the water tightness of the funnel covers and boiler room ventilators. Despite this, Cdr Herbert accepted the submarine on behalf of the Royal Navy providing the submarine was dry docked to check for damage from the grounding. While the boiler room was pumped out and ventilated, the crew had lunch aboard the Comet, a small tender. Mr. Cleghorn and Mr. Macmillan, Fairfield directors, were put ashore, Mr. Macmillan had to make arrangements for the docking. After lunch, the crew prepared the submarine for the test dive.

Lt Cdr Herbert turned K13 towards the head of the Gare Loch and ordered "Diving Stations". As the submarine prepared to submerge, he walked aft along the superstructure to pass the order down the open engine room hatch. When he got to the control room, he took the periscope and ordered "Dive to 20 feet". Almost immediately, the people in the control room realised that something had gone wrong. The depth gauges showed that the vessel was sinking far too quickly and, more worryingly, there was a sudden increase in the air pressure. A report was received that the boiler room was flooding. Lt Cdr Herbert immediately gave orders to blow all tanks and to put planes to rise, all watertight hatches were shut and the for'd drop keel was released. In spite of this, the submarine continued to sink. Lt Cdr Mitchel on E50 thought 'she dived quickly'. A maid working in the Shandon Hydro Hotel, Annie McIntyre, reported seeing two people in the loch, who called out, then disappeared, but, at the time, her claims were dismissed.

Mr. Hepworth, the Admiralty Electrical Overseer, was in the Boiler Room passage when the submarine began to dive. Through the bull's eye in the side of the compartment he saw water pouring into the Boiler Room. Initially he rushed into the engine room and then back through the passage towards the control room to report this. He was one of the last men to get through the watertight hatch between the passage and the amidships torpedo room. Mr. Struthers, the Fairfield Assistant Manager for the K13 build, was the last man through before the hatch was shut; in fact, the closing of the door was delayed a few seconds to give him chance to get through. Two men were trapped in the amidships torpedo room.

Three voice pipes from the stern compartments to the control room and their isolation valves were shut as quickly as possible, but, to make matters worse, before this could be done a jet of water from one of the pipes sprayed the switchboard. This caused several short circuits which in turn blew fuses and caused a fire in the cables. The control room quickly filled with white choking smoke from the burning insulation. A sack was hurriedly pushed into the voice pipe to stop the rush of water until the valve was closed.

The submarine came to rest on the bottom of the loch in 65ft of water, with a slight list to port and an inclination of about 4° up by the bow.

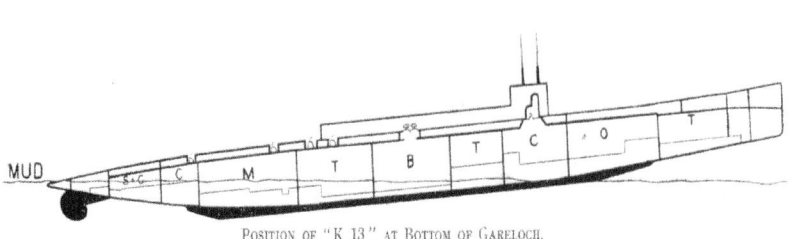

WL   WATER SURFACE.

MUD

POSITION OF "K 13" AT BOTTOM OF GARELOCH.

The obnoxious smoke irritated the eyes and throats of those trapped, complicating even the relatively simple procedure of passing orders, as most were having difficulty hearing due to the sharp rise in air pressure and the choking smoke made it difficult to speak. The burning cables were at the back of the switchboard and anybody attempting to smother the flames with wet sacks risked getting electric shocks. A chart table drawer was hurriedly smashed and some time was spent extinguishing fires by poking wet sacking on to the burning cables by means of splinters of the drawer bottom.

Numerous telephone calls to the engine room went unanswered which lead those in the control room to believe that everybody aft had perished.

After the attempts to blow the fwd tanks there was little air left in the air banks. Luckily the batteries were fully charged and could be used for lighting, pumping and running the air compressors. The compressors were run for a short time to reduce the pressure in the boat and ease the pain in the survivors' ears. Unfortunately, this reduced the pressure on fwd bulkhead of the Boiler Room and although the bulkhead bore the extra load, the leak rate increased.

As the valves that controlled the flooding and blowing of the aft tanks were in the Engine Room, the crew remaining in the Control

72

Room were unable to blow any water or oil out of these tanks. For the same reason, the after-drop keel could not be released.

The outlook appeared to be desperate, and probably all those on-board thought they had little hope of ever getting off the submarine. Mr. Hepworth said to Percy Hillhouse, "This looks like the end" and Hillhouse could only agree, "I am afraid it is." Coxswain Moth said he wouldn't have minded losing his life in a fair fight with the enemy, but this was a "rotten" way to die. There was no panic, only somber faces and restrained conversation.

The submarine had dived at 3 o'clock and those on-board thought the alarm would be raised at about 3.30; it would get dark at about four o'clock. It was likely there would be no contact with the surface until daybreak on Tuesday morning, in 17 or 18 hours, providing the survivors could survive that long, and there were no further incidents. E50 was conducting diving trials in the Gare Loch and the Captain Mitchell had been watching K13 dive, and he "did not like the look of it." He dropped a buoy to mark the spot where she dived.

After this, he sailed over to the Comet and discussed the matter with Mr. Cleghorn, who was also worried about the large quantity of air which appeared on the surface. After a brief discussion, Mr. Cleghorn went ashore to telephone Fairfield, and inform them of the potential incident.

As luck would have it, it was almost high water when the submarine sank so they didn't need to sail too far from the shore to find water deep enough for diving. Pilot Duncan thought that the submarine had settled upon clean hard gravel. The weather was calm and the loch smooth and sheltered. The incident had happened very close to the greatest shipbuilding and engineering centre in the world, and soon all resources of the Clyde yards would be made available to help rescue the submarine. The submarine was low on compressed air, but the battery was fully charged and the lighting was reduced to a minimum.

On Monday evening Sir Alexander Gracie, KBE MVO, the Chairman of the Fairfield Company, had received telephone calls from the yard and by Captain Morris, the Glasgow Harbourmaster. Both informed him that "something" was wrong with K13, but neither were able to tell him what that something was. He immediately contacted Captain Bartelott, Captain Superintendent Clyde, who was unaware of the accident. He then got in touch with the Fairfield directors at the Shandon Hydropathic, a hotel at Faslane overlooking the Gare Loch. They told him that the situation was very serious, so serious that they felt his presence was urgently required. The yard car was sent for but unfortunately the company driver, Mr MacDonald, was not at his home and had to be found, and it was about eleven o'clock before Sir Alexander and Captain Corbett, assistant to Captain Bartelott, were picked up and it was midnight before they reached Shandon.

There they found that the Gunboat "Gossamer" and the Submarine "E50" were standing by the scene of the accident and that the crew of the "Gossamer" were grappling for the sunken vessel. She was located about 2am. The Gunboat had a diving suit, but no diver, so the company car was sent back to Fairfield to collect the company's diver. At about four o'clock the diver arrived, but on his first descent, the suit, which had not been in use for several years, developed a leak. Luckily, he wasn't too deep and he was quickly brought back to the surface. Once again the car was sent back to Fairfield to bring a diving suit, and once the diver made his descent, contact with the sunken submarine was established.

During the rescue operations, the firm's car traversed the distance between Shandon and Fairfield no fewer than 14 times and covered altogether about 400 miles.
Percy Hillhouse

After the submarine settled on the bottom the survivors began to open the watertight doors to obtain more room and more air.

74

They very cautiously opened the watertight door between the Control Room and the amidships Torpedo Room. This allowed the two men who had been trapped in the Torpedo Room back into the Control Room. The torpedo room was practically water free, although the after bulkhead, which was designed to withstand a pressure of 15lbs. per square inch, but due to the present situation the pressure was nearer 25lbs., was leaking freely and a considerable quantity of water was coming through the voice pipe, the glands for cables, telegraph shafting etc.

One of the clips on the forward side of the door between the officer's quarters and the forward torpedo room had accidentally fallen down when the door was shut. As there was no one forward of the door, the clip could not be lifted and the door could not be opened. The clip was not tight and the door could be pushed slightly away from its seating, but not enough to reach the clip. For about two hours Messrs. McLean, Struthers, Green and Bullen worked on the door, after stripping all the rubber packing off to allow a little more play on the hinge side, the clip was raised with a bent wire.

The accomplishment of this successful piece of burglary was greeted by a ringing cheer.
Percy Hillhouse

The water was rising about 2 feet per hour in the amidships torpedo compartment, and this was controlled by running the electric bilge pump for short periods.

Mr Hillhouse calculated that with the air the forty eight survivors had available to them, they would last eight hours unless the air could be replenished. The air lasted for about forty two hours, the survivors were able to bleed some of the compressed air supply. At intervals Mr. McLean bled a small quantity of air into the torpedo room and at the same time forced air back into other bottles by using the air compressor. On Tuesday, the air was so bad that a struck match would not light. As the air became increasingly foul it became progressively difficult to breathe. Due to the increasing carbon dioxide levels the survivors' breathing became painful and the rate increased. Even the simplest of tasks became difficult. Some found just standing was easiest, although Captain Duncan, the pilot, walked to and fro in the Control Room for a lot of the time. Most, however, were generally inactive and apathetic. They lay down where ever they could, half asleep, half awake and breathing noisily. The few available bunks had two or three occupants and the armchair was in great demand also. A few even tried to rest on the deck under the wardroom dining table; they were less likely trodden on.

And so the long night passed away.

At day break, at about 8 o'clock on Tuesday morning, the survivors could see a greenish light through the periscope.

Some specks on the glass gave the illusion of a light green sunlit sea with a man rowing in a small boat, and it was only the immobility and constancy of the picture that assured us of its unreality. Through the bull's eyes in the sides of the conning tower we could distinctly see the wire guard rail which ran around the topsides
Percy Hillhouse.

At the time of the accident the hydraulic system, which worked the periscopes and the wireless masts, was running on the after pump, that was in the Engine Room. This was disconnected, and with the help of a half-a-crown which was a blank flange, it was changed over to the forward pump.

I understand that the lender, being a Scotsman, ultimately got his money back, upon the plea that he wanted to keep it as a souvenir.
Percy Hillhouse.

The survivors raised the periscope to indicate their position. Unfortunately they learnt afterwards that they had not broken surface. At about this time the survivors' heard heavy footsteps and tappings on the outside of the hull. Their general condition was so bad, due to the foul air, that the survivors were practically indifferent to the fact that help was at hand and this roused no enthusiasm, not even a cheer. The survivors returned the tapping in an attempt to establish communication by Morse Code. Unfortunately, this didn't seem to work too well but at least the survivors knew they had been found, and the rescue forces on the surface knew that there were people still alive on-board the submarine.

Occasionally, the survivors had to pump the water from the amidships torpedo room, this was essential to reduce the weight of the submarine and, more importantly, to prevent the water from reaching the batteries under the control room, which would produce deadly chlorine gas.

It was at this time that the Commanders Herbert and Goodhart decided that one of them should try to escape and reach the surface, using the conning tower, and Commander Goodhart volunteered to make the escape attempt. The conning tower was a heavy brass casting that was accessed from inside the submarine through a watertight hatch that opened upwards into the tower. There was an exit hatch with a balanced watertight cover opening upwards into the chart room at the aft end of the conning tower. The forward end of the tower was a dome that housed the projector compass to keep it away from the steelwork of the main hull. Each of the hatches could only be opened and closed from its underside. On either side of the tower was a glass bull's eye, fitted with prisms so you could see ahead, or to the beam.

In preparation for the proposed escape, the vent pipe was removed below the valve, so that by opening the valve, sea water would flood into the conning tower. The projector compass and its tube were removed to make more room in the tower and dome, and the lower portion of the pipe within the control room could be used as a drain pipe to drain water from the conning tower. A flexible hose was attached to the lower end of the pipe and led into the amidships torpedo room. The whistle pipe was broken at a joint and a valve taken from an inboard portion was fitted onto the upper end of the pipe leading from the HP air system, so compressed air could be bled into the conning tower.

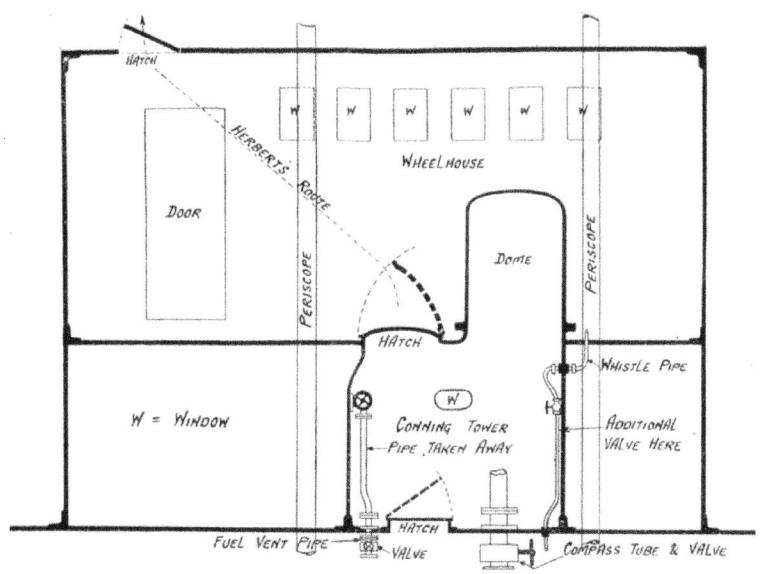

Strangely, one of Commander Herbert's most clear memories of this period is that of a prawn, who had lodged himself against one of the bulls eyes while two Commanders were preparing the tower for the proposed escape. Commander Herbert wrote: -

I can see him still with his little black eyes pressed against the glass; he must have been attracted by the light.

The intention was that both the Commanders would enter the tower and close the lower hatch behind them, which would be clipped from below. They would then unclip the upper hatch, open the sea valve and gradually flood the conning tower. While the tower flooded, the two Commanders would be standing with their heads in the dome, the air could not escape from this. The water flooding into the tower would pressurise the air until its pressure equaled the sea pressure on the upper hatch, the hatch could then be easily opened. The water in the conning tower during the flooding was about three feet deep until the pressure was equalised and the upper hatch could be opened. Once this happened, the tower would flood with an air pocket remaining in the dome. HP air was then turned on, the intention being that, helped by its rush to the surface, Commander Goodhart would escape via the upper hatch and swim to the surface. Once he left the tower, Commander Herbert would shut off the air, shut and clip the outer hatch and knock loudly on the inner hull, an iron rod was left in the tower for this purpose. This was the signal to open the drain valve and once the water stopped flowing from the drain pipe, the survivors would unclip and open the lower hatch so Herbert could climb back into the submarine.

While the tower was being prepared, Mr Hillhouse's hydrometer case, a small tin cylinder, was prepared to carry a message to the rescue forces in case Commander Goodhart's attempt failed. The cylinder was wrapped in red bunting and carried a written account of the survivor's condition and instructions to their immediate needs. Commander Goodhart would carry the cylinder and release it as soon as he was clear of the wheelhouse, it would then float to the surface. Many of the survivors wrote farewell messages to their next of kin, and these were placed in the cylinder. A list of survivors was also enclosed.

Both men were ready and I can picture now, as I am writing this, these two brave officers. Two of the bravest men it is possible to meet. What a picture, Goodhart was dressed, in his shirt, pants and sea boots and Herbert was dressed in his shirt, cap and sea boots. The sea boots were worn on my advice, knowing that he was to come back into the boat and also knowing how difficult it is for one to keep his feet when standing in water, unless he is weighted, at the feet.

Goodhart carried in his hand a sealed tin tube, in which was a message, saying how we were placed, and also saying what we wanted. The last thing we heard Goodhart say was, "If I don't get up, this tin tube ought to".

Herbert now said, "I think everything is ready now", "I think we will try". He then took off his wrist watch, which he handed to the second Coxswain, at the same time making this remark, "I might ask you for that later on"

Cox'n Oscar Moth

The two Commanders removed most of their clothing and climbed into the conning tower closing the lower hatch. In the control room they clipped the hatch, opened the air valve and waited. After a short while they heard a rumbling, gurgling sound which meant that the upper hatch had been opened.

In the Control Room they waited for the pre-arranged signal, the banging on the pressure hull that would be the signal to open the drain valve. But the gurgling continued and no signal was heard.

Eventually they had to shut the air valve and hope that both Commanders had somehow managed to escape

We afterwards learned that the two Commanders had opened the sea cock and had stood till the ice-cold water had reached their middles. Their ears were drumming and deafened by the high pressure of the air, a thick fog filled the upper space and rendered the electric light useless. Then the door was lifted, air turned on, Goodhart said, "Well, I'm off," and with Herbert's "Good Luck" in his ears, dipped under the water level in the tower and passed up through the hatch.

Herbert stepped forward to close the hatch, but the rush of the expanding air was so great that in spite of himself he was forced

upwards through the opening and into the wheelhouse, and then by pure good luck, was carried by the escaping air aft and up through the hatch in the after-end of the wheelhouse roof. He partly swam, and was partly carried by the ascending air, to the surface, breathing most of the time and brushing aside the "wireless" wires as he passed.

He came up close to the diver's boat, and the diver, who was standing with helmet off on his ladder, grabbed him and helped him on-board.

Herbert's first words were, "Where's Goodhart?" and we can imagine his horror when he was told that he had not appeared.

Percy Hillhouse

The tin cylinder failed to reach the surface. It was found in the wheelhouse along with the body of Commander Goodhart, who appeared to have been stunned when his head hit the wheelhouse roof, after being swept upwards by the escaping air.

Despite the amount of equipment available, rescue efforts were hampered due to a lack of information about the conditions on board the stricken vessel. Important facts were missing, such as the number of survivors and their condition, who were still alive and could they assist in their own rescue? It was also unknown in which part of the submarine they were sin or what angle the vessel had come to rest at. Another important question was what had caused the accident and equally as crucial, how much of the submarine was flooded, had salt water reached the batteries and did the survivors have light. So, it was a stroke of luck when Commander Herbert surfaced, that he was able to give the rescue party definite details as to the survivors condition and to advise as to the best means of assistance. For over an hour he refused to dress or see to his own needs, until he was happy that the rescue forces had the necessary information and equipment in place to attempt a successful rescue

Somewhere around 11am I saw a great commotion in the water, just like a pot boiling. I knew it was air escaping that was causing it and it was such a volume that I thought they had at last managed to release the Drop Keel Blocks on the keel and that the ship was freeing herself but my conclusions were wrong. It was no such luck, for, in the midst of the commotion, a man's head and shoulders suddenly appeared. It was Commander Herbert. His first words to us, before we pulled him into a boat, were "Have you seen Commander Goodheart?" and, of course, we had to say "no". He replied "Well, he should have been here. We both left the submarine together."

Captain Herbert was clad only in a shirt and a pair of socks, a very scanty dress for the icy cold waters of the Gareloch in the month of January. Poor Goodheart failed to come to the surface, for, in making the attempt to escape, his head had come in contact with a beam and he had perished. The escape was made through the Conning Tower Hatch. Herbert got clear but Goodheart had missed the opening. In less than a quarter of an hour, Commander Herbert was out working like a Trojan in a suit of borrowed clothes. His help and advice was invaluable. He gave us an indication of how may men were alive, their actual position and how things were in general in the interior of the vessel. It had been decided upon, after consultation inside the submarine with the officials and leading ratings, that the two Commanders would try to come to the surface to give the rescue party the data they so badly required.
Fairfield Foreman Tam Ney

Often I have been told. "It must have been a terrible time for you" and as often I have replied, "Yes, but not so bad for us as for those on the surface upon whom rested the responsibility of getting us out". The news had spread like wildfire over Glasgow and the surrounding districts, and though no word appeared in the press, it was the one subject of conversation.
Percy Hillhouse

At this time, until the diver reached the stricken submarine on Tuesday morning, the only things the rescue forces knew for sure were that K13 had dived and not surfaced and she was probably not lying at the bottom of the Gare Loch by choice!

Until the diver reached K13, the Fairfield directors and staff had little sleep that night and the Captain Superintendent and his staff were also hard at work. By dawn, divers and craft of all kinds were at the scene, and Captain Young, a salvage expert, and his famous salvage vessel "Ranger" were on their way from Holyhead. From the start of the war, Captain Young RNR) was appointed HM Naval Salvage Advisor. His ship "Ranger" was loan to the Crown, and became one of the HM Salvage ships.

By chance HM Salvage ship "Thrush" was at Greenock, having just completed the salvage of the "Mavisbrook" at Loch Maddie. She sailed for the accident scene at 6am on Tuesday. She was accompanied by a number of other vessels, including two Clyde hopper barges and a trawler. Admiralty Salvage Officer Kay RNR was in charge of the salvage operation. He placed wire ropes under the bows of the submarine and attached them to the two Clyde hoppers on one side and the Salvage vessel "Thrush" and to the trawler on the other side. Captain Young relieved Kay when he arrived on the scene soon after Commander Herbert escaped.

Many ideas were discussed on how best to effect the rescue. The first object was to save life, and thereafter, to salvage the vessel herself.

Mr John Lipton, a member of the Fairfield Drawing Office staff, arrived at Faslane on Tuesday morning. He was in charge of the piping arrangements of K13 so he was very familiar with the external air connections and other services' connections external to the hull. He brought all the relevant plans with him and on meeting the rescue forces, quickly suggested that an armoured hose should be fitted to the existing forward high pressure air connection and a second hose should be attached to the forward ammunition hand-up. He chose these hull openings as both could be shut off from inside the submarine. This recommendation undoubtedly had a major influence on the outcome of the rescue mission. Mr Lipton returned to Fairfield yard to collect the required adaptors and hoses. A diving bell was also sent from Fairfield, but this wasn't used. Scotts Shipbuilding and Engineering sent Mr Hugh Leitch and Mr West, both familiar with the K-Class submarine, by tug boat to the accident scene, to see if they could be of assistance. They had with them a roll of plans and various tools, hoses, and other equipment they thought might be of use, and arrived at Shandon about 6 o'clock. They were told that everything that was required was already on site, and much to their regret, they had to return to Scott's without having been able to render any assistance. Before leaving, they were asked not to move the engines of the tug boat for some time, as messages were being tapped to and from the survivors within the submerged vessel.

During the discussions regarding the possible rescue options, it was thought that, if, as appeared probable, the submarine was too heavy to be lifted, then the crew must be brought up without the submarine. To this end, a rescue tube was suggested and the necessary instructions reached Fairfield just after clocking off time on Tuesday evening, when workers were leaving the yard.

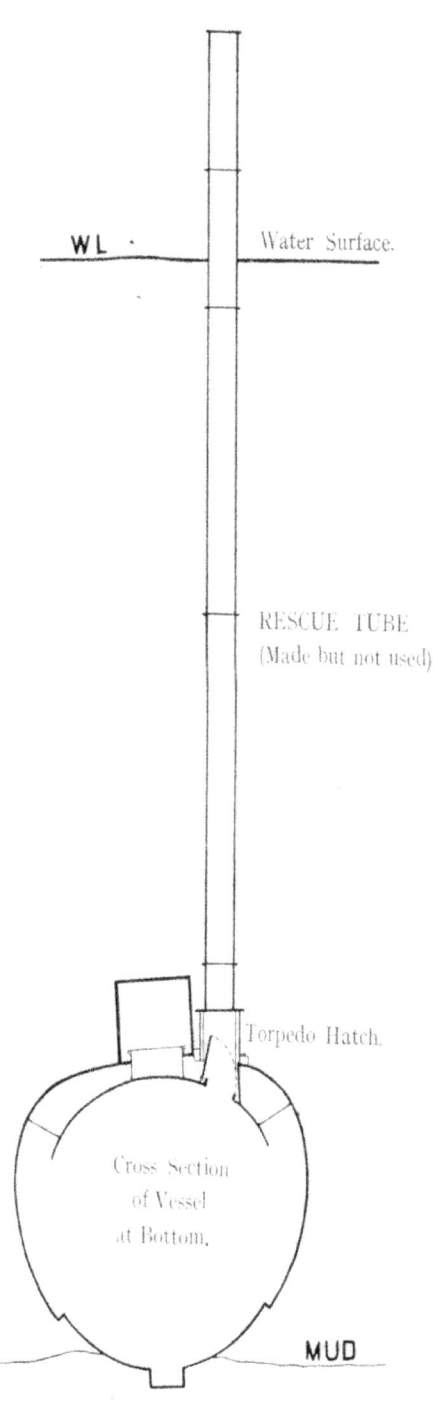

WL ·   Water Surface.

RESCUE TUBE
(Made but not used).

Torpedo Hatch.

Cross Section
of Vessel
at Bottom.

MUD

Staff were quickly recalled and soon Mr. Hendin, the Fairfield Chief Draughtsman, and his drawing office staff were at work. At 8pm on Tuesday night they had produced working drawings for the proposed steel tube, which would be 27 inches wide and 60 feet long, with a box at one end, that would fit over the outer hull forming a watertight seal over the midship torpedo hatch. This would be fixed in place by divers and guyed to the hull. A discharge pipe ran from the lower end of the tube to the surface. The top would be temporarily sealed by a bolted plate. Once in position, the water in the tube would be forced up the discharge pipe by air. (See Diagram 4) The cover could then be removed so that a member of the rescue team could be lowered down to the submarines casting and get the survivors to open the torpedo hatch. Then, one by one the survivors would be hoisted to the surface.

The problem was that the rescuers did not know if the survivors were able to open the hatch or even lift it. So, they thought they might have to cut a hole in the cover with an oxy-acetylene burner, a very unpleasant and dangerous task for the worker involved.

Our foreman caulker went to the man who he hoped would take the hazard and said to him casually,

"Someone will be wanted to go down that tube and cut a hole in the hatch; who do you think would be the likeliest man for the job?"

"What's that you say?"

"I'm saying do you know any man likely to be game to go down the tube with a flame and cut a hole in the torpedo hatch?"

And the answer came, "I'll do it; but you've an awful funny way of asking."

Percy Hillhouse

All through the night the ironworkers and carpenters worked on the tube, box and pipe and by eleven o'clock on Wednesday morning the structure was completed, three hours later it was at Shandon. The tube was never used.

During the time we were so busy in the Gareloch, the Fairfield yard, Govan was also busy constructing and building an escape shaft or tube. A squad of men under the leadership of the late Tom Paul, Iron Manager, worked night and day without rest to complete it and sent it down to us but it never got past Helensburgh. When I was told by Mr McMillan, Managing Director, who was on the spot all the time, that such an escape tube was coming down, I just could not see how it could be fitted to the vessel. The vessel was in 98 feet of murky water. Time and tide was the greatest factor in the men's salvation. Steadying such a tube, keeping it in position, drilling holes to fix it, keeping it watertight and then cut a hole to let the men have access to it, would all have been challenging tasks and if the water got into the Battery tanks, it would mean that gassing would take place and it would gather a volume of water in the

erection that we could not get rid of. It was utterly impossible to attempt to do anything with it. In theory, in the drawing office bench, it was alright but in the murky, swirling waters of the Gareloch, it would be a different matter. I think the idea was Sir Alexander Gracie's and some Naval experts. On a puffer on the way up to Helensburgh, I explained and pointed out all these difficulties to Mr McMillan and I was delighted to hear him say "You are quite right, Dey. It can't be done." And he ordered it to be returned to the Yard without even taking the castings off it. It was a good job we had a man with the experience and the courage to condemn what his boss and so called Naval expert had created. Recently, I read in the Glasgow papers of a diver who claimed to have fitted a shaft on K13 and thereby saved 40 lives. It was an untruth. I have no recollection of him being nearer the scene than at least 20 miles away.
Tam Dey, Fairfield

At about 6 o'clock on Tuesday evening the survivors were informed, by Morse code, tapped on the hull, that an HP air supply had been connected to the submarines air system. There was a pipe from the air system that went through the pressure hull, it was used for operating the guns. To enable the air bottles to be recharged from the shore or from another vessel, a flexible air pipe had been connected.

The survivors slightly opened one of the joints in the system and cautiously opened the inboard valve. Unfortunately, all that came out of the pipe was sea water mixed with a few bubbles. They caught this water in buckets, hopeful that the water would stop and they would get to the air. But eventually they had to close the valve and try to tap out a message to tell the surface forces the attempt had failed.

A diver disconnected and examined the air hose. He found that the cause of the problem was a blank flange that had been fitted, effectively sealing the pipe. After this was repaired the survivors cautiously opened the valve and this time there was rush of pure dry air. Some of the air was allowed to escape into the hull, then the joint was made tight and they proceeded to charge the air bottles. Now it was about 4am on Wednesday morning, the survivors had been trapped for about 37 hours. At this time the diver hung an electric lamp in front of the lens of the periscope, the rescue forces could use this to send messages to the survivors but unfortunately they couldn't answer.

I expect a good many of my readers will be asking why the air wasn't pumped into the boat to breathe? Well the reason is this, inside the boat we already had a tremendous amount of pressure, but there was no means of telling the amount, as we had no barometer to measure it. We ran our low pressure compressor from time to time to take air out of the boat, but after a bit we considered it unwise, for the simple reason we didn't know whether we had taken the pressure down to normal or not. Of course, we found afterwards that there was still a tremendous pressure, but we thought it wise to leave things as they were, for the present at any rate.

Another reason we didn't use the L.P. compressor is that it is run by the same motor which runs the Ballast pump, and we needed the pump very badly. This motor can either be clutched into the compressor or the pump, but only one thing can be run at a time, and as the pump was most needed, we kept it clutched in, the best part of the time.

Our biggest trouble was the watertight bulkhead between the boiler room and the beam tube room. This was leaking very badly, and it will easily be seen why it did leak. This was only a collision bulkhead and was tested to a pressure of fifteen pounds and as we were below seventy feet, the pressure on the bulkhead would be thirty-five pounds, so we must think ourselves very lucky it held as well as it did.
Oscar Moth

At about 5am, the bottle groups were fully charged and they began to blow out all the forward tanks, the seven foremost external tanks and the internal tanks forward of the Boiler Room.

As they had no means of knowing when these were emptied they had to guess how long to keep the blow on each. As the air bottles were fully charged, they made reasonably sure that each was completely blown before they blew the next tank. They nervously watched the bubbles of the fore and aft spirit levels for signs that the bow was lifting, but for a long time nothing happened, the bubble remained motionless at $4°$ up by the bow. They had almost given up hope when the bubble moved! There was a shout of delight as they watched the indicator move slowly to $5°$, $6°$, $7°$, $8°$, $9°$, $10°$, and that was as far as it could go. As the bows lifted the wire cables, which had been passed under the bows from the salvage vessels, slackened, they were immediately tightened to keep the bows in position. The angle of the decks became steeper, until the rescue forces saw the bow rise out of the water. They signaled for the survivors to stop blowing unless the escaping endangered the diver.

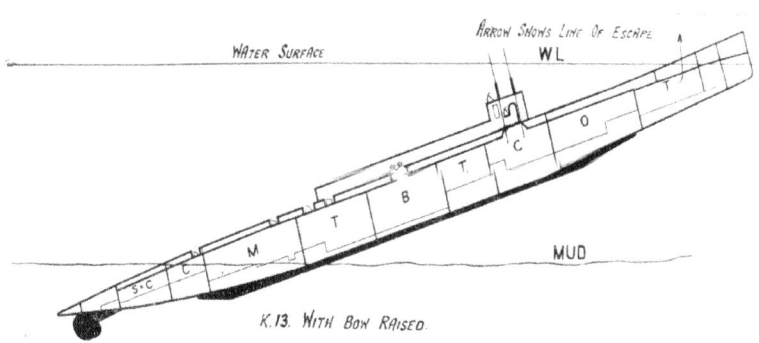

K.13. WITH BOW RAISED.

Now the submarine lay with her stern approximately 12 feet deep in the mud, and her bow about 10 feet above water, the angle of inclination was about $16°$. Although this does not sound particularly steep, it was very uncomfortable for the survivors to move about, especially as the deck was covered by greasy linoleum.

Many unpleasant falls were experienced and the unfortunate who came down usually made a non-stop trip to the end of the

compartment, accompanied by as many of his friend as he could conveniently gather into his arms on the way! I remember standing near the forward end of the Officer's Quarters holding a chain which hung from above when my feet were knocked from beneath me by someone involuntarily going aft in a sitting position, and I was left swinging on the chain.
Percy Hillhouse

Through the periscope the survivors could watch the rescuers as they attempted to save them, they could even recognise some of those aboard the surface vessels.

Apart from the problems it caused moving around the submarine, the steep angle caused another inconvenience. Due to the inclination of the submarine the bilge pump was now so high that it was unable to pump the water from the after end of the torpedo room. The survivors were very worried that the water would enter the control room and reach the batteries. They started to bail this water in buckets and carry it to one of the forward bilges.

This was a very slow and tiring procedure, the survivors had but two buckets at their disposal and one of them leaked. The steep angle of slippery deck only compounded the problems. The survivors formed a line, each man held himself in place by one hand and passed the bucket with the other. The bailing continued until Mr. McLean and Mr. Bullen had the idea to take the cover off the manhole for the tank under the Torpedo Room, this allowed the bilge water to run directly into the tank. When the tank was nearly full, the manhole was closed, and the tank was blown, discharging the water into the loch. The manhole was then re-opened and the process repeated. This had the added benefit of replenishing the air. Each time the manhole was opened the compressed air, that was used to blow the tank, escaped into the fwd spaces. By using this method, the survivors were able to keep the water level well under control and it never came near to the batteries. For some reason there was some confusion and for a time the rescuers believed that the batteries were in imminent danger of being flooded.

Now we had another very anxious time for our pump lost its suction and refused to pump water from the beam tube room. This was very serious indeed, for the water began to gain rapidly. Our hearts began to sink once more and we had to pass water in buckets forward to a place where the angle of the boat helped the pump and at last we got it to suck again. I can picture the exhausted men passing these buckets of water, for what in normal times would have been, an easy task, now was a very heavy one, and it was as much as a man could do to lift a small bucket of water.

Oscar Moth

Another rumour which gained considerable currency and credence may be here disposed of. It was said that we passed away the long hours by playing cards. I can assure you, and I have no doubt you will readily believe, that no one felt the least desire for such an occupation. There were cards on board, but they were never used. I still have two much-discoloured packs which were taken from the vessel in a very sodden condition after she was raised. The story probably arose from the fact that after we had got fresh air, food and liquid, and as we began to nurse a faint hope of ultimate rescue, our spirits revived wonderfully, and in reply to a question from above as to whether we would like anything else to be passed down the tube some joker replied, "Nothing but a pack of cards." It was also rumoured, and by some believed, that the Captain had been shot out of the torpedo tube with such force that he landed in Row. (Rhu)

Percy Hillhouse!

At this time a further connection was made to the hull. There was a seven inch ventilator and hand hole that passed through both inner and outer hulls in the Officer's Quarters. This had a screwed cover on the casing and a hinged cover in the submarine.

The diver removed the top cover, passed it to the surface where a hole was cut in it and a four inch flexible armoured hose was securely attached to it. The cover was then replaced and most of the water sucked out of the pipe by means of a smaller suction hose. Word was then passed to the survivors, by tapping on the hull, to open the hinged cover. As they did this, a large amount of water drained from the opening. Once this stopped, the air began to rush out of the submarine. The air pressure in the vessel was still considerably above that of the normal atmospheric pressure. The escaping air was so black and foul that the rescuers were amazed that anyone could still be alive.

An unfortunate consequence of the reduction of the air pressure within the submarine was that the leak rate through the boiler room bulkhead increased. Luckily, the bulkhead did not collapse due to the additional load caused by the reduction of air pressure on its forward side.

The survivors could now talk directly with those trying to save them. They immediately asked about Commander Herbert. They thought Commander Goodhart had reached the surface, but Herbert had been trapped in the conning tower. Much to their relief Commander Herbert replied himself. It was not till much later that the survivors learned that Commander Goodhart had lost his life in the escape attempt.

The diver had found explanation of the disaster by discovering that the four air inlets to the boiler room were fully open. These should, of course, have been closed before the signal, "Engine room closed" was set in the control room, but by some oversight this had not been done. The accident was thus due to no defect in the design or construction of the vessel, but to a momentary forgetfulness on the part of someone who paid for his error with his life. When the vessel was ultimately examined, the lever controlling the air inlet covers was found to be standing at "open".
Percy Hillhouse

Besides making communications easier, the four inch tube was large enough to pass down small items and soon a small bottle of brandy appeared, dangling on the end of a string. This was served in the brass cover of an electric switch.

One member of the crew declared that it was the first time he had ever touched spirit. I think that even the most rabid teetotaller would agree that the occasion was ample justification for so tremendous a lapse.
Percy Hillhouse

The rescuers then sent milk and chocolate through the handhole. No one was particularly eager to eat; before the accident a number of sandwiches had been brought on-board, these were passed round about 6 o'clock on Wednesday morning although very few were eaten. Survivors were more thirsty than anything. Their throats and mouths were parched and dry, undoubtedly as a result of the quality of the air they had been forced to breathe.

At intervals throughout our imprisonment we were alarmed at the sudden burning out of fuses, one of which would flash and spit and jump out of the switchboard every now and again, and the lights it had been serving would go out.
Percy Hillhouse

A high pressure air hose had been passed down the four inch flexible hose and was passed round the foreword compartments forcing out the stall air. The survivors gathered round the hose and breathed in lungfuls of refreshing and reviving fresh air. Never had the survivors appreciated the value of fresh air so much.

But so soon do we take our ordinary blessings for granted that a little later we all wanted that hissing air pipe removed as far as possible from whatever part of the ship we were in, as its noise was insupportable. "Take that beastly pipe away up forward, shove the damned thing aft" - anywhere except where it was.
Percy Hillhouse

The survivors began to feel better as the hull filled with fresh air and the foul air was expelled through the flexible hose and they began to speak again, although they all felt that at any minute some further mishap might befall them and send them back to bottom of the loch. All the time during their imprisonment the survivors had in the back of their minds the possibility that they might have to move from the control room if the boiler room bulkhead showed signs of failing. Mr. Skinner and his team spent a lot of time rewiring electric wires so that they would be independent of the switchboard and of the after battery under the control room. The bulkhead held so these arrangements were not required. Unfortunately, while connecting a wandering lead to the starter of the air compressor, one of the men accidentally made a short circuit which blew the main fuse and plunged the whole interior into darkness. The last 6 hours of their confinement were spent in total darkness. To light the forward compartments, they only had one wandering lead from the switchboard, two magazine hand lamps and one electric torch.

Now that the submarine's bows were above the water, there was still the problem of getting the survivors out. Initially it was hoped they could exit the submarine by one of the bow tubes, but the bows were too low in the water and when the survivors carefully opened the inner tube door, they found the tube was flooded, they had no choice but to close the tube.

Next it was decided to try and pump the water out that was between the pressure hull and the casing so a hole could be cut in the forecastle deck and another directly below it in the pressure hull. The survivors were told it would take about 20 minutes to pump the water out and then the hole would be cut, using an oxy-acetylene cutter, a few minutes later.

The survivors assembled forward and started to prepare the compartment for the proposed escape. The rescuers intended to cut the hull above the forward ballast tank, and the survivors spent a considerable amount of time removing the nuts from the

94

manhole cover on the tank. This would have been a difficult escape route; each man would have to wiggle through the manhole and then would have nothing to stand on while climbing through the hole in the pressure hull. Eventually it was decided to cut the pressure hull just aft of the tank bulkhead, the hull, which at this point, was deeper under the water, but the escape route was much easier. The survivors removed the wood lining, then gathered on top of the torpedo tubes, waiting for the first signs of the cutting flame.

Soon the promised 20 minutes had become an hour.

"When are you going to start cutting?" they called up the voice pipe.

"In about a quarter of an hour," the rescuers replied. "We are pumping hard and there's not much water left."

The quarter of an hour seemed to pass very slowly.

"Have you started cutting yet?"

"No, not yet, but we will be ready in a few minutes more, there's only about six inches of water left and we've sent for a larger pump."

The time seemed to pass even slower. They sat in total darkness, talked quietly and passed the air hose around. Everyone was now confident that they would soon be free but could not say so in case it somehow jinxed the rescue attempt.

I cannot remember how often I traversed the slope between the group forward and the voice pipe to put the query, "When are you going to begin cutting?" nor how often I carried back the "Quarter-of-an-hour" reply.
Percy Hillhouse

But unfortunately, the water level in the interspace didn't seem to be dropping, it appeared that just as fast as the hand-pump was removing water, it was flowing back in. At this stage Commander Herbert queried the position of the flap valves, he suspected that the flaps were leaking. In fact, he was preparing waterproof plaster to be used to block the flaps. The survivors were asked to confirm the position of the flaps, which were controlled from on-board the submarine. These had been opened for the diving trials but had been shut by a crew member before pumping began. Mr. McLean checked the flaps and found that one of the valves had been left partly open

The casing is a light structure which had openings just above waterline, this allowed the casing to flood and drain when the submarine dived and surfaced. In order to avoid these holes allowing water to enter when the submarine was steaming on the surface, flap valves were fitted and these were opened or shut by hand wheels in the submarine.

The water level dropped quickly and after a few minutes the interspace was clear. The hole was quickly cut and Lieut. Singer gave the order "Civilians first". There were loud cheers from the men on the rescue vessel as the survivors climbed out of the submarine. Forty eight men were rescued, each one being welcomed with noisy applause which could be heard in the Control Room by those still waiting their turn to escape. The last man to come out was Lieutenant Singer, who along with Mr. Wallace and Mr Hillhouse, had carefully closed the watertight doors behind them as they made their way forward.

It was a weird scene which met my eyes as I emerged from the superstructure. It was about 10pm on Wednesday night - 55 hours after our dive - the moon was full and amid a bunch of vessels of all kinds illuminated by cluster lamps and crowded with staring faces rose the snout of K13 set at an absurd angle, with a black square hole on its surface from which the last survivor was being helped to freedom and life.
Percy Hillhouse

The survivors were transferred to small motor boats and taken to the shore, then escorted through a double line of spectators to Shandon Hydropathic Hotel.

I think the crowds were a little disappointed that we were so fit; they would have dearly liked to have had the pleasure of carrying us up. I was taken charge of by two good folk, whose names I will never know, and in spite of my protestations that I was quite able to walk, I was carefully guided to the door of the Hydro.
Percy Hillhouse

At the hotel the survivors were given a warm welcome. Hot baths and supper were ready for them and they could contact loved ones and tell them the good news, using the telephone and telegraph. Captain Duncan, the Clyde pilot, much to everybody's amusement, sat himself down in front of the fire reading a newspaper, not taking part in any of the discussions about the incident. When asked about apparent indifference, he replied that he hadn't seen a paper for three days!

Heavy steel hawsers were passed under the submarine to help raise her bow and to hold her in position. Due to the water slowly leaking into the hull, the strain on the hawsers became too great and at about 6 o'clock on Thursday afternoon, the bollards were torn out of the supporting barge and K13 sank.

One of the housemaids from the hotel, Annie MacIntyre, said that she had been on the shore in front of the Hydro on Monday afternoon and had seen two men swimming in the loch, who shouted "Oh!" and then threw up their hands and disappeared. She mentioned this to several people but they did not pay much attention to her story, people assumed she had been mistaken. When it became known that the diver had found the engine hatch open, people were more inclined to believe her story. When the bodies were finally recovered from the submarine, two were found to be missing, Lt A Lane, the submarine's engineer and Mr John Steele, Foreman, Engineer from Fairfield. Lt Lane's body was found about two months later, Mr Steele's body was never found.

The salvage operation started on the 2 February 1917, the aim being, to recover the casualties who were trapped in the stern section and to get the submarine back to Fairfield to be refitted.

As the submarine hull was intact and deeply embedded in the mud, conventional salvage methods could not be used. It was therefore decided to shut the Boiler Room intakes and the Engine Room hatch, then air hoses would be connected into the upper part of each of the nine compartments. Air pipes were also connected to the ballast and fuel tanks. Discharge pipes, which would allow water to escape from the hull, were positioned close to the air pipes. They were fitted with control valves so the pressure in the hull could be controlled and the hatches wouldn't be blown off. They also enabled the water expulsion rate to be regulated. Four nine inch wire ropes were slung under the hull to help lift the submarine.

Initially the weather conditions were not favorable, the visibility was poor and the water temperature was practically freezing. The stern of the submarine was buried in about 12 ft of mud and depending on the tide, lay at a depth of up to 80 ft. A Clyde Trust dredger had to be used to clean an area of the seabed to allow access.

Once this was done, the Boiler Room intakes were closed and sealed. This proved to be very difficult. It was necessary to cut the hydraulic pipes and force the intakes closed with screw jacks. The pipes and fittings which had been used to supply the crew during the rescue operation were also removed.

A diving bell, also owned by the Clyde Trust, was used to prepare the submarine for lifting. Several men could work at the same time and this speeded up the work.

An attempt was made to raise the submarine on the 3 March but the stern remained firmly embedded in the mud. Further attempts were made to clean the mud and another attempt to raise the submarine was made on 14 March, this was unsuccessful. A wire rope was dragged under the submarine trying to break the mud suction, but the boat still didn't rise. Air continued to be pumped into the boat and with the aid of the wire ropes, it eventually freed itself and rose to the surface.

The bodies were removed during Thursday afternoon, 15 March, and the morning of the 16 March. They were buried at the Faslane Cemetery during the afternoon of the same day, the 16 March, the Navy personnel in one plot, the Fairfield workers in an adjacent one. Twenty nine bodies were recovered, the two missing were found to be Lt Lane, the submarine's engineer and Mr John Steele, a senior engineer from Fairfield. Lt Lane's body was found further down the River Clyde two months later and was buried with his crew mates on the 9th of May. Mr Steele's body was never found.

After this, the submarine was towed back to the Fairfield yard. A full survey was carried out by Fairfield and Admiralty investigators. Apart from the comments by Hillhouse and Cox'n no official report of the inspection has been found.

K13 was towed by to the Fairfield yard, refitted and recommissioned as K22 and in a strange twist of fate, Oscar Moth became her coxswain.

Commander Goodhart received posthumous award of the Albert Medal for Gallantry, for saving life at sea.

In April, the following letter was received by the Fairfield Company:-

Admiralty, S.W.1
22nd April, 1917

Gentlemen,

My Lords Commissioners of the Admiralty have had under their consideration the minutes of proceedings of a Court of Enquiry held on the 19th ident. to investigate the circumstances attending the accident to and subsequent foundering of H M Submarine K13. I am commanded by their Lordships to request that you will convey to Mr. Wm. McLean, Mr. E. J. Skinner, Mr. F. Bullen, an expression of their appreciation of their services on this occasion, which undoubtedly contributed materially towards the saving of the survivors.

I am, Gentlemen,

Your obedient servant;

(Signed) O. MURRAY.

PART 2

CASUALTY AND SURVIVOR LISTS

When K13 sailed from the Fairfield yard at 0800 Monday 29th January 1917 there were 82 men onboard. 53 RN crew, 16 employees of the Govan ship builder, 5 Admiralty officials, 5 other civilians, a pilot and the captain and engineer of sister submarine K14.

Naval Personnel

Lieutenant Commander Godfrey Herbert, DSO, Captain of K13
Commander Francis H. H. Goodhart, DSO Captain of the sister vessel K14 building at Fairfield - on board to study the working of the ship
Lieutenant Singer, second in command
Engineer Lieutenant Lane, engineer to K13
Lieutenant (E) L. C. Rideal, engineer to K14
Boson H. Pratt, gunner
Petty Officer Moth, Coxswain
48 other naval ratings

55 Naval Officers and Ratings

Admiralty and Sub-Contractors'

F.C. Cocks , RCNC Admiralty Representative
F.W. Searle, Admiralty Overseer
Fred Hole, Assistant to Admiralty Overseer
Donald Renfrew, of Kelvin, Bottomley & Baird
Sydney R. Black, of Kelvin, Bottomley & Baird
William Wallace, Director, Brown Bros, & Co.
E. Hepworth, Admiralty Boiler Overseer
W. U. Hancock, Admiralty Electrical Overseer
Edward Powney, Chadburn's Representative
Robert Lake, Brotherhood's Representative
Joseph Duncan, Pilot

11 Admiralty and Sub-Contractors

Fairfield Engine Department:-

John Steel, Foreman
William Lewis. Leading Hand
William Strachan, Leading Hand
William Kirk, Leading Hand
Donald Hood, Leading Hand

6 men

Fairfield Shipyard Department: -

William McLean, Manager of Submarine Department
E. J. Skinner, Manager of Electrical Department
Frank Neate, his Assistant
William Struthers, Assistant Manager on K13
Frank Bullen, Assistant Manager on K13
John Green, Head Foreman mechanic
Percy Hillhouse, Naval Architect

8 men

On board at time of diving were: -

55 Naval Officers and ratings
11 Admiralty and Sub-Contractor's men
16 Fairfield Officials, standing by only, the ship being worked
entirely by her own crew

82 Persons in total.

Mr. Cleghorn and Mr. Macmillan, Fairfield directors, were put ashore, Mr. Macmillan had to make arrangements for the docking. That left 80 personnel on board the submarine for the test dive.

List of Casualties

Royal Naval Casualties

Officers

Commander Francis Herbert Heaveningham Goodhart
Lieutenant (E) Arthur Ernest Lane
Bosun Herbert Pratt

Ratings

PO Frederick Raymond Porter, DSM 171745
AB Robert William Williams J3706
CERA Frederick William George Smith 270355
ERA 3rd Class Tom Bradley 272472
ERA 2nd Class John Arthur Roberts 1629/EA
Chief Stoker Walter Abraham Fensom 297570 (Ch)
SPO George William Fieldwick 301111
SPO George Jenkins Williamson 229331
L/Sto Thomas Mitchell 302275
AL/Sto Stephen Clutson Clark K5824
L/Sto Frederick James Howard K9207
Sto George William Bevis K8719
Sto Herbert Cornish K9219
Sto John Dickinson K11895 (Po)
Sto Ridgeway Dymond K14330
Sto Henry Charles Goddard K20432
Sto Timothy Hallihan K12408
Sto Richard Hooper O/N K9871
Sto William Lovell Roberts K1715 (Dev)
Sto Alfred Scarlett O/N K/12902
Sto Horace Simpson O/N K4303 (Dev)

Sto Leonard White O/N K15229

Civilian Casualties

Frederick Stephen Hole, Admiralty Overseers Assistant

The Fairfield staff killed in the accident are commemorated on a memorial drinking fountain erected by the Fairfield Company in Elder Park, opposite the site of the Fairfield Building Yard on the Clyde.

John P Steel, Fairfield Engine Department
William Chalmers Smith, Fairfield Engine Department
William John Lewis, Fairfield Engine Department
William Alfred Strachan, Fairfield Engine Department
James Kirk, Fairfield Engine Department
Frank Thomas Neate, Fairfield Foreman Electrician

List of Survivors

Royal Navy Survivors

Officers

Commander Godfrey Herbert
Lieutenant Paris Graham Singer
Lieutenant (E) Leonard Chichester Rideal

Ratings

CPO Reginald Atkinson O/N 233659
PO Robert Oscar Moth 220366
PO Robert William Nicholls 195631
PO Stanley Albert White 220128
L/Sea Charles Frederick Osborne 225038
L/Sea Robert Henry Hudd 231390
L/Sea Arthur Travers 238252
AB James Patrick O'Regan 238673
AB Frank Harry Byrnes J5561
AB Albert Knight J373
AB Arthur Henry Kirk 235218
AB Henry John George Akers 195047
AB Ernest Edward Stevens J5146
AB Henry William Frederick Mackrell J26655
AB Richard John Pring Wattley J16437
AB Robert Young J10983
AB Thomas Arnold Guthrie J8959
AB George Edmondson O/N 228678
L/Sig Arthur Reginald Riley J21077
L/Tel Charles Albert Harry Freestone J15536
Boy Tel Joseph Swift J44055
ERA Owen Charles Lewis M3716
CERA Albert Denne M4470
SPO Charles Smith 302886 (Po)
Sto Ernest Alfred Smith K19554

Sto George Baker O/N K7178

Civilians

Frederick W Searle, Admiralty Ship Overseer
Edward Hepworth, Admiralty Overseer (Boilers)
William Hancock, Admiralty Overseer
Robert Lake, Brotherhoods Ltd
Frederick C Cocks, RCNC
Prof. Percy Hillhouse, Fairfield Chief Engineer
Edward Skinner, Fairfield Electrical Department
William MacLean, Fairfield
Donald Hood, Fairfield
Frank Bullen, Fairfield
John Green, Fairfield Mechanical Foreman
Henry Kerr, Fairfield
William Struthers, Fairfield
Edward Powney, Chadburns of Liverpool
Donald Renfrew Kelvin, Bottomley & Baird
Sidney Black Kelvin, Bottomley & Baird
William Williams, Brown Brothers (Boilers)
Captain Joseph Duncan, Clyde Pilot

PART 3

THE ACCIDENT POSITION

There has been some confusion regarding the actual position of the submarine sinking. During 2017 Mr Gerry McFeely, as part of his research for his Centennial Paper, determined the actual position.

He discounted the two "internet" co-ordinates and studied some Twenty different written sources on her depth when she came to rest on the seabed. He also had a photograph of K13 being raised in the Gare Loch, taken 31 January 1917. This was then subjected to a geometric and topography analysis and the Naval Photography Department from HM Naval Base Clyde imposed 1917 photo onto a current photograph of the Base taken from the same area and angle. Finally, the Hydrographers of the Chart Maintenance Unit at Faslane plotted all the cardinal points onto both the 1922 and 2015 Admiralty charts.

The actual position of the sinking was 56 degrees 03 minutes 05 seconds N / 04 degrees 49 minutes 05 seconds W[imperial].

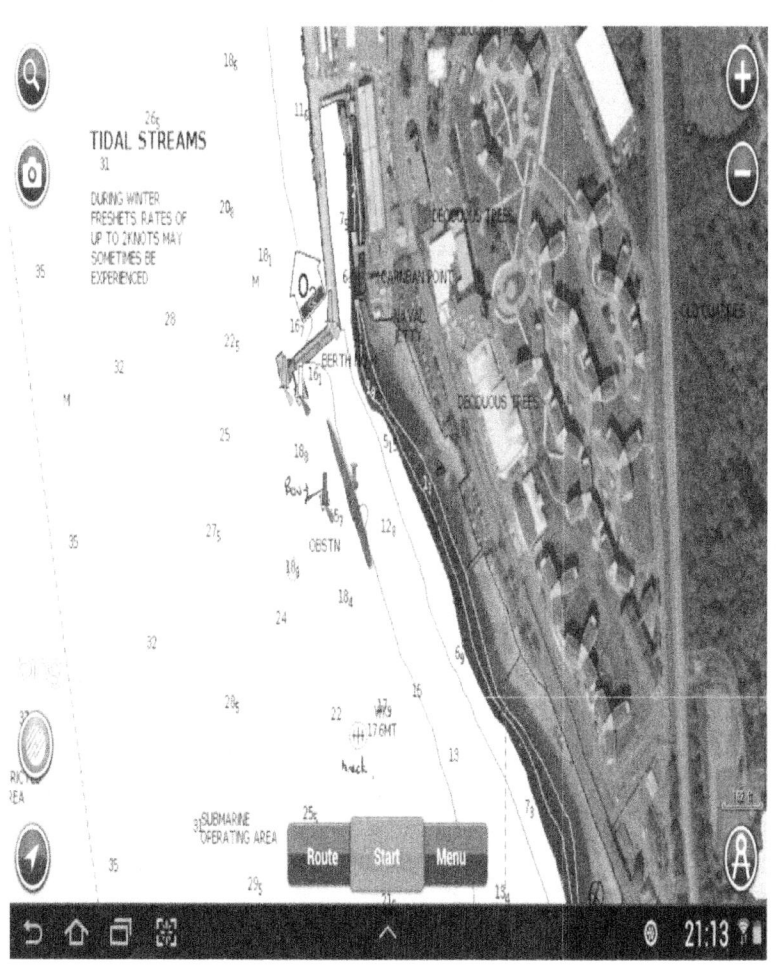

The accident position

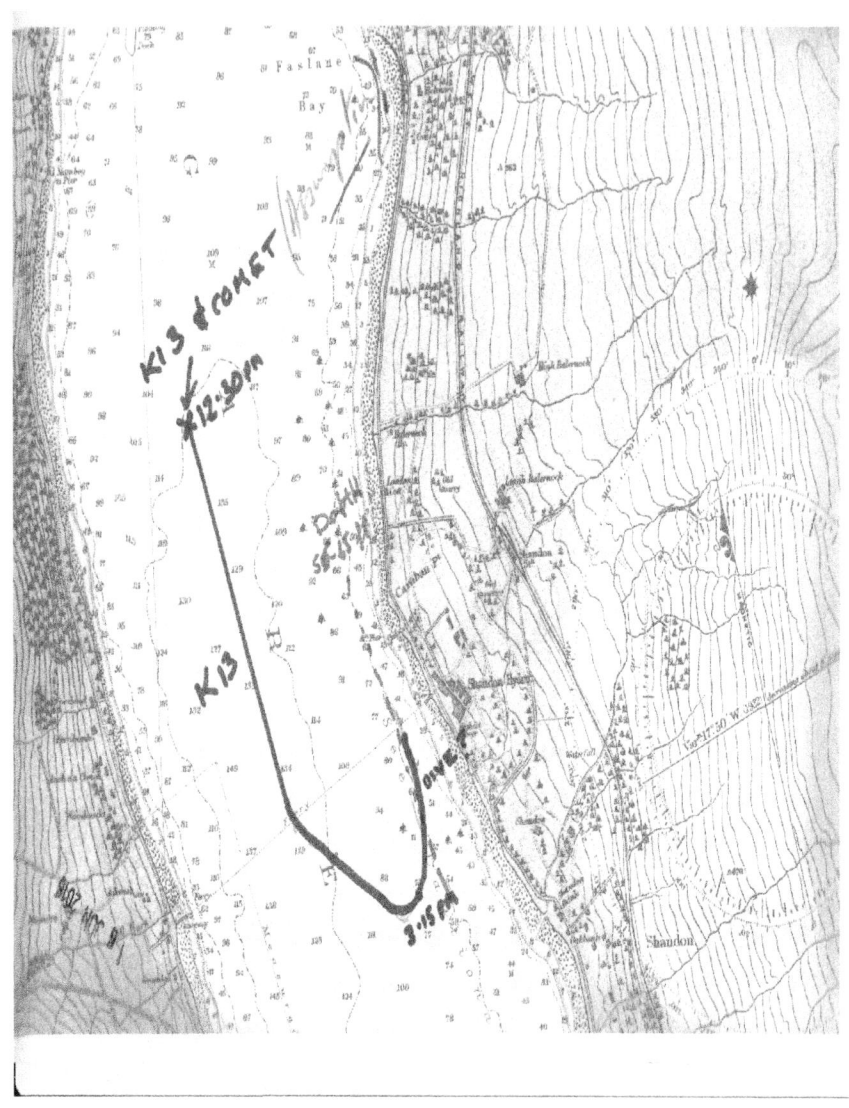

The submarines track before the accident

K13's bow's raised to the surface. The present HM Naval Base
Clyde's jetty is overlaid on this picture, to show how close to the
shore she was.

CHAPTER 3

THE BOARD OF INQUIRY

The Admiralty Court of Inquiry was held in the Board Room of the Fairfield Shipbuilding & Engineering Company, Glasgow, on Monday, 19th February, 1917, to enquire into the circumstances attending the foundering of Submarine K13 in the Gare Loch on Monday, 29th January, 1917.

PRESENT: -

Acting Captain Godfrey A. Corbett, R.N.P   President.
Commander Aubrey T. Tillard,   H.M.S. "Firedrake"
Commander Ferdinand E.B. Feilman,   H.M. Submarine K14,
Commodore Captain Sydney Hall,   Admiralty Adviser.

Witnesses called:

Lieutenant Commander G. Herbert, D.S.O

Lieutenant Paris G. Singer, K13

Lieutenant (E) Leonard C. Rideal, K14

Petty Officer R. Moth, Coxswain K13

Frederick William Searle, Admiralty Supervisor

William McLean, Submarine Manager at Fairfield

William Struthers, Assistant Manager on K13

Edward J. Skinner, Manager of Fairfield Electrical Department

William Hancock, Admiralty Electrical Overseer

Percy A. Hillhouse, Fairfield Naval Architect

Lieutenant Commander G. Herbert, D.S.O., the commanding officer of K13, was the first to be called. The Board had before them a statement written by him, regarding the incident:

Fairfield Yard
Govan
3rd February 1917

Sir,

On Monday, the 29th January, I proceeded to the tail of the bank, and after carrying out various trials on the surface proceeded up the Gareloch for Diving Trials. About noon I dived the boat to 80 feet for about 15 to 20 minutes to test the water-tightness of the hull; the after Beam tube in particular which was quite dry. On rising to the surface, Engineer Lieut. Lane reported that there was a small leak in the Boiler Room but owning to the heat there he was unable to find out exactly the cause. Accordingly, he asked me to dive again after he had ventilated the Boiler Room. This was done for half an hour during which time all hands went to dinner. About 3 p.m. I ordered Diving Station, and after remaining on the superstructure abaft, the Bridge Shelter until the funnel doors were clipped down, proceeded to the Conning Tower where I received the report from Lieut. Singer, (1st Lieut.) that the Engine Room was shut off. I ordered flood all externals and headed the boat up the Gare Loch, and as soon as she was steady, ordered Dive to 20 feet. I watched the bows through the periscope, and simultaneously with their going under water I received a message from the Engine Room from Eng. Lieut. Lane to come to the surface as the Boiler Room was flooding. I gave the order "Surface blow 2 & 3". There was by this time a very considerable rush of air from aft which indicated that there must be a large in rush water so I ordered close all W/T doors. The depth gauge showed 35 feet with 4° inclination by the bow. I stopped both motors and proceeded to blow every tank possible but with no effect. Great difficulty was experienced in shutting off the voice pipes through which large quantities were coming, and the Main fuses blew in quick succession which indicated that the Motor Room was flooded.

The boat was quite tight everywhere except that the beam tube room made about 1 foot an hour which was easily kept down with the Forward pump. I consulted Mr. Hillhouse, Naval Architect, and he gave me no hope of raising the bow even though the forward tanks were empty. Commander Goodhart and I were of the opinion that there was nothing to be done until the diver found us, and then although getting air and food down nothing short of blowing off the after part of the boat would bring us up.

During the night we heard sounds as if someone was trying to locate the ship, with a grapnel, and at about 6 or 7 a.m. we reported to the divers tapping, but could get no sense with the Morse Code. During the forenoon I asked Commander Goodhart if he would try and get out at low water, 12.30 p.m. With the necessary instructions to those on top for giving us air and food.

Accordingly, after thinking things out, Commander Goodhart decided to try for it and I agreed that I should try and close the door after him. I arranged code of signals to Lt. Singer in order that he could drain down the Conning Tower after Commander Goodhart had gone clear.

Commander Goodhart & I worked all forenoon taking away the projector compass to give headroom, and also in connecting an H.P. valve to the whistle pipe to act as a blow. When everything was ready, I charged the Conning Tower with air, to make sure the bottom door and glands through which electric cables passed were tight. After rectifying this, which took roughly an hour, we were ready.

119

A small tin cylinder about 8 x 1½ inches was then filled with instructions to the people on the surface, and Commander Goodhart, putting this in his belt, proceeded into the Conning Tower with me. His last words were "Well, if I don't get up, the cylinder will". He opened the flooding valves (fuel vent disconnected) and when the water rose to our waists, I turned on the H.P. air. Commander Goodhart knocked off the clips of the Conning Tower. The Conning Tower lid began to let water in and was soon wide open. Commander Goodhart stood up in the dome, took a deep breath, and then made his escape. We were both exceedingly out of breath at the time. Almost immediately I put my hands up to feel for the lid, but without knowing, found myself carried through the opening into the shelter, the roof of which must have struck my head from the bruises and cut I subsequently discovered. All the time H.P. Air was escaping fast from the Conning Tower, and I attribute my escape entirely to this, for, without doing anything I found myself shooting through the the square hatch in the top of the wheel house. I breathed hard all the way to the surface, and fortunately, arrived up between two craft, one of which hauled me aboard.

As soon as possible I sent down a diver to take the cap off the Foremost Ammunition hand-up, and also connect up air lead to the connection which had been fitted on the upper deck for charging the recuperating cylinder of the Foremost Gun.

I gave the cap of the Ammunition hand-up to the Chief-Engineer of H.M. Salvage Ship "Thrush" who, according to my instructions, fitted a 4" flexible steam pipe to it, making a very good job of the same, but it was not until 9 a.m. On Wednesday, 31, that I got into communication with those on board the boat. By this time, High Pressure air had been supplied to the boat through the other connection, so I passed a Diver's air pipe down the 4" hose for breathing purposes; this was followed by various form of liquid food.

During the day every effort was made by those on board to "blow" every drop of water out of all the Forward Tanks. Lieut. Singer was in a very bad way, and was thought to be dying. Mr Searle, Admiralty Overseer, assumed command, and about noon the vessel rose considerably forward. Assisted by the "Thrush", a Trawler and two Hoppers. The bows were raised sufficiently to enable a plate to be cut by the oxy-acetylene flame in the top of the free flooding space just abaft 16 bulkhead. This compartment was then pumped out by hand pumps and finally a hole cut in the main Hull between 17 and 18 frames, through which the crew were rescued.

Lieut. K. Michell and his crew were indefatigable in their efforts, and never rested throughout the operation. The Captain and Officers of the Salvage Ship "Thrush" were particularly painstaking, and I beg to submit that it is largely due to the timely assistance of the various craft which assembled on the spot that the lives of so many were saved.

I deeply regret the loss of my ship and so many of my crew and passengers, including Commander Goodhart, whose efforts to bring news to the surface were frustrated.

I have the honour to be Sir,

Your obedient Servant.

Lieut. Commander

Commodore (S),

Admiralty

All Board questions are in **bold**

Lieutenant Commander G. Herbert was cautioned, he was asked:

By the President - **Will you make a statement of that occurred immediately before and after the accident?**

Yes, but I do not wish to add anything to my official report on the matter at all. One thing I should like to say is with regard to the shutting up of the Engine Room. I put off all externals. I headed the boat up the Gareloch and before the flooding of the externals the men remained on deck, and we were pointing into the shore at the time before I turned the boat up the Gare Loch. There was flooding of all the externals except 4 and 7 on each side.

Is that all you wish to add to your report?

Yes, I kept the four tanks empty till I got straight.

By Captain Hall - **When was the order given to "diving stations" before you turned the boat up?**

Some minutes before.

How was the order passed on?

Down the Control Room and down the Engine Room hatch by myself. I was on the top of the super-structure and I gave the order down the Engine Room hatch. I asked a stoker why he was not at his diving station, and I sent him back.

Would you give the order to flood the externals after you got inside?

Yes.

Did you receive at that time a report that the Engine and Boiler room were shut off for diving?

Yes.

Who from?

From the First Lieutenant.

Had you any means of knowing whether that report was correct or not?

Only the electrical indicator.

Was it showing that they were shut off?

Yes.

Did you receive a verbal report from the Engine Room as well?

No.

On the occasion of the dive before that day, had you adopted the same procedure?

Yes.

You had not been in the habit of receiving a report in addition to the indicator?

No.

So that you relied entirely on the indicator to dive the boat?

Yes.

Did you give instructions to the Engine Room Lieutenant to report verbally in addition to the indicator?

No.

Did you give any orders during the dinner hour as to the opening up of the Boiler Room?

Yes.

What were they?

I told the Engine Room attendant in charge to do what he wanted to - to ventilate the Boiler Room.

Why did he want to ventilate the Boiler Room?

Because of the steam. He had too much steam in the forenoon to enable him to inspect the place for water tightness.

Was there any doubt that they knew that there was a dive on?

None at all.

Are you quite sure that it was shut off during the dinner hour?

I am not certain myself, but I know somebody who saw it off.

How many times had the crew been exercised at the diving stations

This was the third time in reality, and I could not say. There were a good number of times before it left the yard. This was the third time the boat had been under water.

You had given no detailed instructions to the Engine Room Lieutenant as to what procedure he was to adopt?

They had not been given to him at the time. They were in the process of making.

When you went to the diving stations he had verbal instructions what to do? Had you given them?

Yes.

What were they?

To close the funnels and cover the Boiler Room intakes - the ventilators of the Engine Room and the Engine Room hatch - before giving the signal to the Control Room that everything was shut off.

By the President - **Why do you state in your report that the First Lieutenant reported that the Engine Room was shut off?**

Because I was on deck and he was in the Control Room, and it is customary to receive a report from him before coming down from the Conning Tower. On an occasion like this when there was no hurry - I want to say that it was different from a service dive in this way that it was in slow time. I waited till I saw everything, as far as I could see, shut down and the funnels themselves shut up.

Was the report from the Engine Room received from Lieutenant Singer?

Yes.

When you came down would you be able to see whether the indicator was as he reported?

Yes, it was a red light from a conspicuous place in the middle of the room and you cannot mistake it.

A red light indicating that it was shut off?

Yes, it is enclosed in a screen in the Engine Room and "shut off" engraved on it.

By Captain Hall - **How did the Engine Room Lieutenant hear that the Boiler Room was shut off before he reported it as such?**

He gets his information by operating the Boiler Room intakes - a lamp indicating "shut" which shines at the operating position.

Does he receive a report in addition to the second Petty Officer in the Boiler Room?

Presumably, yes. I had not given him instructions. Very often you cannot stay in the Boiler Room when it is shut off and everyone quits the Boiler Room at once.

By the President – **Even if he were in the Boiler Room could he readily see the indicator?**

Not without climbing up on the top of the grating.

By Captain Hall - **Is there not a special indicator for the express purpose of showing that?**

It is not down on the platform at the furnace doors.

But it is in full view of the Stoker-Hold?

Yes.

By Commander Tillard - **You had taken over the boat from the contractors and had entire charge?**

Yes, I was entirely in charge and with Naval Ratings.

<u>By the President</u> - **Were the civilians merely representing the firm?**

Yes.

<u>By Commander Feilman</u> - **Had they plenty of time in the Boiler Room before you prepared to dive after you gave the order "diving stations"?**

Yes - ample time - five or six minutes.

<u>By the President</u> - **That is supposing that the Engine Room Lieutenant received your message?**

We had lunch together, and it was to his benefit the whole time, and I sent him down to be ready to go to diving stations.

Had you told him personally to get ready to dive?

Yes.

<u>By Commander Feilman</u> - **Could you easily see whether the vents were closed?**

Quite easily.

And you dived specially for that purpose?

Yes, especially to see if these vents were tight.

<u>LIEUT. PARIS G. SINGER, K13</u>

<u>Called and Cautioned</u>

<u>By the President</u> - **Will you state to the Court what happened just previous to your diving so far as you know as to the facts?**

I am not very clear as to the intervals of time.

Can you give us a general account of what happened?

I came over from the "Comet" and there was an order "diving stations". The funnels were being turned down just then, and I sang out to tell them to delay. They were just going to dive. Someone waved his hand and went down the Engine Room hatch. I went down through the Conning Tower into the Control Room and saw all the necessary hydroplanes and motors running, and as soon as everything was ready for diving I saw that the lights in the indicating room were shut off. I reported to the Captain, and I forget exactly the orders that were given. When the Captain came down he asked if the Engine Room was shut off, and I reported to him that it was. The lights were turned on again and he gave the order to flood externals, and then in a minute or two minutes to dive to twenty feet. The first time I noticed anything wrong was the pressure of air in the ears, and at the same time I was standing near the voice pipe and I heard through the voice pipe "surface, Boiler Room flooded". I sang out, I forget the exact words, but I said "surface, Boiler Room flooded". I do not remember the exact sequence of two or three orders. Then I heard "close water-tight doors", and I immediately saw that the air was in the tanks. I went back to see that the water-tight doors were being closed. I also gave the order to drop the keel forward. I went back to the water-tight doors in the after-Control Room, and one of the indicators was the wrong way, and it would not shut. It was just then that the main motor fuses blew. The door was shut and I went forward to see that the keel was dropped. I think that was all.

Will you state, not in - detail, but roughly, what happened from that time onwards till you were rescued?

The first thing that I was occupied with was shutting off the voice pipes and seeing that the after water door in the main Tube Room was shut, and then the shutting off of the voice pipes (as the water was coming over) and stopping the fires.

Were the valves closed?

The voice pipe cocks were all open and the fires were put out and then we set on to get the pump running as they were making water in the Beam Tube room, and as we go the pump running we kept the water down.

Where was the water making?

In the Beam Tubes. It was coming in through the glands in the bulkhead and the voice pipe connections.

Did the water come in all the time that you were down there?

No, sir, by that time we had a list to port and 4 degrees up from the bow.

By Captain Hall - **When you got the orders "diving stations" did you get them direct from the Captain?**

No, they were given when I was at lunch.

Do you know how they were passed over?

It should have been by voice pipe.

You were not down below when the orders "diving stations" were given?

No.

Did you receive any order as to the indicator?

No.

Had you any personal knowledge of the procedure adopted at the after part of the vessel when "diving stations" were ordered?

In the Engine Room?

Yes?

I knew that it had to be shut off.

Had you laid down the stations?

Yes.

What stations had you laid down for the diving stations to the Engine Room?

I had laid them down to the engine room.

Did Engineer Lieutenant Lane lay them down entirely?

Not entirely, I helped him a little.

Had the engine room Lieutenant laid them out to all his people in the Boiler Room and the Engine Room and in the Motor Room?

Yes, as far as the people looking after these were concerned, and I assisted him in that.

But the actual Engine Room rating and the Boiler Room were arranged by Engineer Lieutenant Lane?

Yes.

Do you know what these were?

I did know, but I cannot remember them all now.

Do you know whether it included the report which they had as a check on the indicator?

No.

You never enquired on that point?

No.

Had you previously reported the Engine Room and Boiler Room to the Captain entirely on the electrical indicator?

Yes.

How many times had you exercised the crew at diving stations?

I took them at the dinner hour every day.

Twelve times?

Yes, quite - more than that.

You tried to use Fessenden when you first went down?

Yes.

Would it work?

No.

Was there any water in the Engine Room passage?

No.

Was there much after the accident?

Very little.

Did you take complete charge?

Yes.

Until when?

1 do not know how long after it was till I took ill and Mr Searle took charge after I got ill.

Would you like to say anything as to anybody in particular down below?

No. I saw Mr M'Lean and Mr Bullen more particularly.

Can you tell when your externals were finally blown?

Not very well, but I heard the bubblings outside.

Can you tell on this occasion when two and three were blown?

No.

Right off?

No, it was when we started.

Were they well up?

I did know, but I do not remember now.

Did the Engine Room Lieutenant of K14 come in and report to you?

He did not report to me.

No report of any kind?

No.

Did he make any statements as to the condition aft?

Afterwards when things were quietened down.

Before you were rescued?

Yes, he did, but do not remember clearly what he said.

Was he quite unaffected by the accident?

Yes, as much as anybody else.

By Commander Feilman - **When you were ill why did you not turn the boat over to Lieutenant Rideal?**

He had very little submarine experience, and he also seemed ill.

You did not think that he was competent to take charge?

He did not know the boat as intimately as I.

LIEUTENANT (E) LEONARD C. RIDEAL, K14

Called and Cautioned -

By the President - **Will you state to the Court what happened from the time the order was given to dive up to the time when you arrived in the Control Room?**

I did not hear the order to dive at all. I came down through the Control Room and went into the Engine Room and Lieutenant

Lane was working the funnel operating gear. He finished that and then I went over to the Boiler Room vent indicator on the port side. I noticed the lower one. The lower light was flickering and it looked to be showing the vent opening. I asked Lieutenant Lane about that and he said it had been connected up the wrong way round, and nothing further was done. He then gave the order to close down the Engine Room hatch. I did not see that done because I was looking forward at the time and he sent the Chief E.R.A. to see if they were making any water. The Chief E.R.A. came back almost at once and reported that there was a good deal coming in and he closed the door after him. As soon as the Chief E.R.A. had come out of the Boiler Room I saw the water coming through the exhaust pump which leads through into the Boiler Room, and Lieutenant Lane was at the starboard one. I then decided to come through and tell the Captain what was happening. As I was coming through into the Control Room Lieutenant Singer was just closing the door into the Control Room, and I reported to Commander Goodhart what had happened in the Engine Room.

Did you notice if anyone was standing by the telemotor gear for closing the vents?

There was an E.R.A. during the forenoon trials, but I did not notice him at the afternoon trials.

Can you say who worked the telemotor gear for closing the vents on that afternoon?

I cannot say.

By Captain Hall. - **Were you fully sensible of the fact that you were about to dive?**

I knew that we were going to dive when I came down from the deck.

But when you were in the Boiler Room?

I did not hear the motors going; I did not her them starting.

But did you know that you were about to dive?

No.

<u>By the President</u> - **What made you ask the question about the vents being closed or not?**

Because I saw the light flickering and knew that Lieutenant Lane was about to dive and I knew that the vents were being closed. I was not aware that he had dived.

When you were in the Engine Room alongside the Engine Room Lieutenant of the ship, did you know that preparations to dive were being made?

Yes, I did.

Did you hear any report made to the Engine Room Lieutenant from the Boiler Room that the Boiler Room was shut off for diving?

No.

Did you not expect to hear one in view of your doubts about the vents?

I had my doubts about the vents and that was what made me speak to Lieutenant Lane about them.

Were you quite satisfied with his reply?

I thought it rather unusual.

Was there any light showing in the lamp to indicate "Vents closed"?

I do not remember any other light except the lower of the two lights which certainly was flickering "Vents open" and that was the one that attracted my attention. The others in the room were right, but I saw the lower one flickering, indicating "Vents open".

The other lamp was not showing anything?

I would not make any statement about the other lamp. These lights are about 8 inches apart.

By Captain Hall - **Was there any possibility of your mistaking the thing being open or shut by these lamps?**

If they are connected up the wrong way.

But if they are working correctly?

Reading "Vents open" or "Vents closed" - I do not remember whether the upper light was burning or not. I would not make any statement about the upper light.

Were you in the Engine Room or Boiler Room after dinner?

No, I came out as soon as it was over.

By Commander Feilman - **You saw these lights flickering when they were shutting off for diving?**

Yes.

And you pointed that out to Lieutenant Lane?

Yes.

Did he do anything about it or go to the Boiler Room to see?

I did not notice him doing anything. He was apparently satisfied that the vents were closed because he told me that they had been connected up the wrong way round.

<u>By Captain Hall</u> - **On the first occasion of diving did you notice the vents?**

I would not make any definite statement whether they were or not.

Did you hear the order "Diving stations"?

No.

Did you see the Engine Room Officer put his switch over?

No, I did not.

Was there any water in the Engine Room when you left it other than that coming through the ventilator?

I could not be sure. 1 thought that it was coming through the ventilator.

Was it quite clear to your mind what had happened?

I was only under the impression that the Boiler Room was flooded.

Was there any water in the Boiler Room passage when you left it?

No, there was none.

Was it just after that that you experienced the pressure of air?

I did not experience any air pressure till I got to the Control Room coming through the passage. I did not notice any draught or anything the matter, but after I left the Control Room I noticed that the pressure was greater than normal.

<u>By the President</u> - **Do you know if Lieutenant Lane was aware of the cause of the flooding?**

No, I do not know.

Did you hear him making any remark before you left the Engine Room?

No.

Do you say that Lieutenant Lane was quite aware that the boat was diving?

Yes, I think he was, because he sent the Chief E.R.A. to see if she was making any water which he would not have done had he not known that we had dived.

<u>PETTY OFFICER R. MOTH, K13</u>

<u>Called and Cautioned -</u>

<u>By the President</u> - **Will you tell the Court what happened from the time that the Captain gave the order to dive or "Diving stations"?**

When I got the order "Diving "stations" I was on the upper deck and the crew were at the diving stations in the Control Room and I waited till further orders. All the crew, as far as I am aware, were at the Diving Stations.

What happened then?

The order was given to flood the tanks and I was told to go down. We dived the boat and when she was showing between 10 and 11 feet on the gauge the air pressure came into our ears and I heard someone say something about "Hard to rise: Close water-tight "doors". It was put hard to rise and there was no control over the boat and we had to blow tanks.

After Lieut. Commander Herbert had left the ship whose orders were you following?

I followed anybody's orders that was in authority, but I really think I placed myself under the Admiralty Overseer's orders.

All the time?

Yes. Anybody who had authority over me.

But you looked upon Mr Searle as being in authority?

Yes.

Was there any overseer?

Yes. The Engineer was doing a lot of things, blowing tanks, and superintending a lot, but I considered that the Admiralty Overseer took practical charge.

How did the crew behave?

As a whole they behaved extremely well.

You had no case of panic?

None at all, sir, at any time.

FREDERICK WILLIAM SEARLE.

Called and Cautioned.

By the President - **You are the Admiralty Overseer in Fairfield?**

Yes.

Will you tell the Court if your responsibility with regard to overseeing this ship included the boiler vents which are in question? –

Well, I took on myself to do with the telemotor system and I thoroughly examined it on the Sunday and I put the system under a 2,000 lbs pressure and kept it there. I tried every valve in the boat, not once but several times.

Do you know of your own knowledge that this gear was all right on the day that it was being worked?

Yes. I knew for a fact that Lieutenant Lane spoke to me about these ventilators and he asked me if I would come and have a look at them. He said that he thought one ventilator was slightly sticking when being opened.

Was this after dinner?

No, this was in the morning and I came on deck with him and the port after ventilator was about three-quarters of an inch up and not fully at the stops, and since I was able to explain why that would happen I did not worry.

But they were working correctly?

Yes.

Did you work them from the Engine Room?

From the forward end of the Engine Room. I did not work them on the day that I was there, but I had worked them before many times.

You did not see them working?

Not from the Engine Room, only from the deck.

How could you tell they were working?

Because they must be open or shut and Lieutenant Lane had told me that he had worked them and this little one was not fully opened. I knew exactly what had happened but after that it was proved conclusively that the four could be opened hard on the stops. They were there at lunch time between the first and second dives.

How do you know?

Lieutenant Lane came into the Boiler Room, but I am not a good witness for this. During the lunch hour Lieutenant Lane had opened these vents to cool the Boiler Room as much as possible, so that really what we intended diving for in the afternoon was a leak and he wanted to cool the Boiler Room, and he sent his Chief E.R.A. to see whether these vents were wide open then. I did not hear the E.R.A come back

Did you hear the order "Diving stations" being passed?

Yes.

Where were you?

In the Control Room.

Did you see the indicator show the Boiler Room shut off for giving?

No, I did not. That was one of the points that I did not look at myself.

I understand that you took charge practically of the vessel when the Commander left the boat?

Not exactly. I could not tell you the exact time but it was when I saw that Lieutenant Singer was very ill and someone had to take charge. I spoke to Lieutenant Singer and asked him if he had any objections that someone else should take charge, and so I did so.

Were you satisfied with the way that your orders were carried out?

Absolutely.

Did the crew behave well?

Yes, they did all that I asked at all times.

Had you ever tested the indicators of the Boiler Room vents or seen them tested?

I had not personally tested them, but I had seen them worked.

Do you consider it possible for the Boiler Room vent handle to be worked with the stop valve shut, so that the officer would think that he had been closing the Boiler Room vents when in reality nothing was happening?

Yes, I do think it is possible. I myself have often worked the handles of these vents when there has been no pressure and I thought that there was pressure, and I had to go back and slacken the pressure. There is one invariable way of telling, there is a

142

pressure gauge. Every time you work the handle you can see it taking up the pressure and anyone can make the handle go back again.

Was that pointed out to the crew?

Yes, to my knowledge. It was absolutely pointed out to the men in the Control Room who work the whole of these vents.
The Boiler Room vents? –

Personally I do not know whether it was pointed out to the Boiler Room but it was to the Engine Room.

You did not yourself point it out to anyone there?

Not as a separate trial in the Boiler Room. As a whole everyone in the boat knew it but with regard to the Boiler Room vents I do not think I pointed them out particularly to anyone.

LIEUT. COMMANDER G. HERBERT, D.S .0. Formerly examined -

Called and Cautioned

By Commander Hall - **Did you have this pointed out to you, the Boiler Room vents being worked with the stop valve shut?**

I knew it.

You do not know whether Lieut. Lane knew it?

No, I should like to say one thing, that I was continually speaking about the tightness of the stop valves on the telemotor system.

Had you at any time had any dealings with these Boiler Room vents?

None beyond inspecting them.

FREDERICK WILLIAM SEARLE, Recalled

By Commander Hall - **Was there a pressure gauge at the pump?**

Yes, but that was away from the control. I do not think there was a pressure gauge at the control.

Can you tell by the handles whether the valve is open or shut?

Yes, you can tell that, but there is no difference in the feel whether you have pressure on it or not.

But you quite know, of course, that the intakes are open and that the stop valve is shut off?

Yes. We keep the pressure on the system in order to ensure that there is a pressure keeping these things open.

If the stop valves are not shut are the intakes very liable to close?

There would be a liability to close through the pressure in the system.

Is it not the fact that they would close?

No, I would not say for certain.

Would you expect that anybody going there would expect that they would be closed?

Well, answering for the Engine Room, I could not swear, but for all the others I should say that we made a point of always keeping the pressure on our system to keep things open.

Is there an indicator on the stop valve to show whether it is open or shut?

Yes. There is "open" and "closed" marked on them and the direction of the handle.

Is there anything to indicate on these valves whether the valve is open or shut?

No, I would not say that there was anything to indicate whether they were open or shut. There are two letters "open" and "closed" and that would be the direction - merely the letters to show the direction.

<u>By Commander Feilman</u> **- I suppose it is possible if the stop valves were open and if you have the by-pass valve open that you would not have any effect on closing the vent?**

The by-pass being open, you would not keep your eyes on the vent.

And therefore, you could work the lever and you might imagine that you were closing the vent and it would have no effect on the vent at all?

Yes, that is so.

<u>By Captain Hall</u> - **Did the indicators in the engine room show whether they were open or shut in working the lever?**

Yes, they have been worked to my knowledge.

And easily seen?

From the Boiler Room?

Would you like to say anything as to the conduct of Fairfield's people?

Yes, I would very much. I should like here to state that Mr McLean and Mr Bullen were two men who worked like slaves, and there was no rest to them at all. They knew the boat thoroughly and tried everything. They did everything I wanted, and they were ready for any emergency. They were two men who kept in the best condition. At the commencement Mr Skinner was invaluable for the electric work. One is apt to forget what happened during the first hour, but Mr Skinner of Fairfield worked very hard to keep the power on the compressor pump. Brotherhood's men had a representative there who attended to the high pressure compressors to the finish and he was only about 18. Although he was very ill indeed he worked splendidly.

WILLIAM M'LEAN, Submarine Manager at Fairfield.

Called and Cautioned

By the President - **Would you give the Court a description of what happened to your knowledge from the time the order of "diving stations" was given**

I did not hear the order "diving stations" being given, and I was among the last to leave the deck. When I got down to the Control Room, the ship's people were busily preparing for diving and I would not be many minutes in the Control Room when I heard the order passed along that the Boiler Room was flooded. Captain Herbert gave the order to come to the surface immediately and close the external vents and close all water-tight doors. These orders, so far as I could see, were attended to and then the drop keel was let go. None of these had the effect of bringing the ship to the surface and after a few minutes we were settled on the bottom.

Will you give us a brief outline of what happened then?

I may say that at that time I saw the Engine Room light burning and that it was shut off. The Captain had charge of the operations and we tried blowing a few tanks off and pumping in air, but none of these things had any effect. On the Tuesday forenoon the Commander and the Captain had arranged a scheme whereby one of them might get out, but up to a certain point it failed as the Captain of the ship did not return as arranged. Then Lieutenant Singer took charge, but there was very little we could do except to keep the water under with our pump, and we got a change of air as much as possible with the compressor, by taking the air into the compartment and letting fresh air in from the bottom of the compartment.

Were you much excited?

No, none of them were. On the Tuesday we got a connection made on to the H.P. system, but when we broke the joints of the pipe we found that we were getting water only, and it was not till Wednesday morning early that we got a good supply of H.P. air. I cannot tell where it came from, but it came from one of the ships overhead. Then we started charging all the bottles that we had control over back to the Boiler Room group up to an average of about 1500 lbs. After the bottles were charged we continued using air from the shore and blew out little tanks, working from the torpedo room forward. Shortly after starting to blow the midship tanks we found the bubbles moving forward and the ship began to rise at the forward end. Then on Wednesday forenoon we received a 3 ½ inch pipe connected through the ventilator and were able to get into direct communication with the people overhead, and we received a good supply of air for ventilating the ship. I do not know whether there is anything further I can say.

By Captain Hall - **At what time did Mr Searle take general charge?**

147

I do not know that there was any particular time that he took general charge. Lieut. Singer seemed to sink very fast after a while, and Mr Searle was moving about and guiding and instructing us as best he could.

Would you tell the Court if you have any personal knowledge of dealing on the day in question with the Boiler Room vents? –

So far as I know they were working, from my personal knowledge, but not on the day in question.

Did you notice during the dinner hour that the light showing that it had been closed was burning, or not?

No, I did not notice it. I looked at it, and it was burning then.

Had you at any time worked these Boiler Room vents?

Not personally, but 1 had seen them worked.

Have you seen them working by opening the stop valves?

No. I have not seen anyone doing it.

Do you think it easy for anyone to make that mistake?

Yes, it would be quite possible for anyone to make that mistake, especially if they were in an excited condition.

But not under such conditions as obtained on that day?

No, but when we were preparing for diving.

Have you knowledge that the mechanical indicators in the Boiler Room showed that they were shut?

They were only connected on to the hand gear.

Have you knowledge of that?

Any time I was there it was in working order.

And practically impossible for it to be out of order?

Yes, and I never received any complaint about it not being in working order.

EDWARD J. SKINNER, Manager of Fairfield Electrical Department.

Called and Cautioned-

By Captain Hall - **Would you tell the Court if you had any dealings on the day in question that the electrical indicator was working in the Engine Room?**

It comes under me for fittings.

And on the day in question?

There was no question raised regarding the accident. I was not asked about it.

When last did you try it?

It was tried by my foreman during the night and early in the morning.

Was he saved?

No, he was lost. He reported to me that all things were right, both in the funnel and the Engine Room ventilation.

But you did not see them worked yourself?

No, not that morning.

Had you on a previous occasion seen them worked?

Yes, about two days before the ship went down, and they worked quite correctly.

Is it possible that they could have been joined up the wrong way?

No, practically impossible.

You cannot think of what gave rise for anyone saying that they were turned the wrong way?

No, and there was nothing reported to me as being wrong.

Did it come out from evidence that they were joined up the wrong way?

Yes, if the doors went close, they would not shut correctly.

Does not that show that they were open?

Yes, there was a light showing that these doors were open.
On the day in question you had no personal knowledge of the matter?

No.

Was there an indicator in the Control Room showing that they were cut off?

I know the fitting of it and on the day in question it was working. I particularly called Mr Macmillan's attention to it and explained to him how it worked.

Do you know that it was switched off when it came up?

I cannot say.

Can you account for the Boiler Room electrical indicator flickering?

No.

On the occasion of the last time the officer saw it flickering to open, can you explain how that could happen?

There is a connection on the travel of the rod and as soon as the vents made a start to open, before they travelled about a quarter of an inch to half an inch it goes from "closed" to "open" and if they were not closed down hard it would tend to flicker between "closed" and "open".

Would the shaking up of the connection cause that?

They would not change from the one to the other; they would not go from "open" to "closed".

So that the only thing would be the shake in that connection?

Yes.

There is a switch that works the lamp showing in the Engine Room, is that switch marked clearly in the Engine Room?

Yes, it has a plate, not to show whether it is off or on, but it gives instructions that it is switched on when it is shut and switched off when the Engine Room is open.

WILLIAM STRUTHERS

Called and Cautioned -

By the President - **Will you tell the Court what you know of what happened from the time the order was given to dive or to prepare for diving?**

When I went on board about half-past 3 I was in the Control Room, and they had not started to dive and I was not there when the order was given to dive, but I was in the Control Room when the order "diving stations" was given. I knew that the order had been given. I only heard another order when I was in the Control Room by-Lieut. Singer, which was to open all externals. I then went aft to the Turbine Room, and while I was in the Turbine Room I spoke in the Engine Room to Lieutenant Lane, and I also saw him operating the after funnel gear that is on the starboard side of the ship. Shortly after that he said that he did not know whether the Boiler Room vents were closed or not. Shortly after that I asked the E.R.A. who was responsible for the Boiler Room vents, if he had closed the vents and he assured me that he had. I expect that by that time we were diving, because I know that the motor was going. I assumed that we were diving. Lieutenant Lane sent his Chief E.R.A. into the Boiler Room to see how things were and the Chief E.R.A. opened the Boiler Room door and closed it behind him. He was only gone five or six seconds when he returned and said that the Boiler Room was flooding freely. He closed the door behind him and clipped off the door. Lieutenant Lane then said to the man at the voice pipe to tell the skipper to come to the surface immediately as the Boiler Room was flooding fast. Just immediately after that I went forward through the passage to get to the Control Room and there was water coming into the passage when I went through. There were some glands in the after end of the funnel clip gear and I also looked into the bull's eye in the passage and could see that the water was flooding up past there. I got to the other end of the Boiler Room passage between the Torpedo Room and the Turbine Room and one of the service men - I think a reserve man - was stationed at the foot of the ladder and was closing the door at the time. I got through there and got to the Control Room door which was closed. I turned back, and I think it was a torpedo man in the Beam Room who was attending to the door and he shut it behind me. I got into the Control Room, but the water was coming out of the voice pipes. The Captain then asked me if I could get pushed up to the top and turn the voice pipe cock off. I said that the water was putting out the fires and they were blowing the tanks.?

By Captain Hall - **What did you say to Lieut. Lane when you first went into the Turbine Room?**

I had been speaking to him at lunch on board the "Comet", and he told me that he had arranged with the Captain to have another short dive. While on board the "Comet" after lunch we came up on deck and Lieutenant Lane was particularly interested in the Boiler Room vents. He called up to his Chief E.R.A. to go and see what position they were in. The Chief E.R.A. was aft and the Chief Stoker went up on the superstructure and he said that they were full open. Lieutenant Lane was quite pleased with that and that was all right.

Was this after you came on board the submarine?

No. The first time was on the "Comet" and it was when we were on the deck of the "Comet" that he asked the E.R.A. to see. The "Comet" was lying alongside. While I was in the Turbine Room I spoke to him and also the assistant overseer, and I intended to go into the Boiler Room and see if there were any leaks. We were talking about things in general when he said that he did not know whether they were open or not. It seemed as if he were speaking his thoughts aloud. I did not think any more about it at the time, but the place where the vents were was a little congested and there were two or three men there, and I was at the opposite corner. The artificer who was responsible for the job had spoken to me two or three times about operating this trial, and I asked him casually when passing if he had closed the vents, and he said he had, and I did not think any more of it at the time.

Did you see the electrical indicator yourself?

No, I was not at that corner at all.

Had you seen the electrical indicator working that day before?

Not that day at all.

So that you do not know whether it was in order or not?

I cannot say. I cannot say whether it was in order or not.

Do you think that the Artificer, whose duty it was to close the vents, thoroughly understood?

Yes.

Had you worked them with him?

On one occasion he asked me how they operated.

Do you think that he would be likely to operate the lever without opening the stop valve?

I cannot say that he was likely to do it, but that is a thing that might happen with any party, locking them by the opening valve and perhaps forgetting just for an instant in closing the vents.

Do you think that it might be done

It could be done. In spite of the fact that the indicator would not show and if the indicator did not show, then it would call his attention to something being wrong. Still, at the same time, he should have been able to tell when he became familiar with the job and when he pushed the lever the gauge would have shown. There are two pressure gauges, 1,800 lbs., right alongside the lever.

Is the by-pass quite close to the handle?

Yes.

Could that easily have been open so that the pressure would not show?

Yes, it could have been open and the pressure would not show.

Did you hear the Engineer Assistant give any report from the Boiler Room?

No, that apparently had been done before I got that length, because the forward funnel was down and clipped and when I was down he was closing the after funnel and the stokers were waiting orders to clip it. That was done when I was in the Turbine Room.

Did you see anybody close the vents after it was reported that there was flooding?

No.

You had no other conversation with him at that time?

No.

Were you near the Engineer-Lieutenant from K14 when he asked Lieutenant Lane if the boiler room was closed?
No, I did not notice the Engineer-Lieutenant of K14 at that time at all.

WILLIAM HANCOCK, Admiralty Electrical Overseer

Called and Cautioned

By Captain Hall - **Were you on board this submarine on the day of the accident?**

I was.

Where were you?

In the Control department.

Had you any personal knowledge on that day of the state of the electrical indicators working?

No, not on that day.

When had you last seen them?

On 25th January, the day of the final electrical trials.

Were they correct?

They were on that occasion.

Would it be an easy matter for them to be joined up the wrong way?

Not in my opinion.

Would it entail a difference in the length of lead and could it be easily done?

No, certain operations could have been made without any additional lead.

So as to make them show open when shut?

Yes.

But you never saw them so joined up?

No.

Have you any idea how the engineer thought that they were joined up the wrong way?

No.

Had you ever spoken to him on the subject?

No,

Had you ever seen them going wrong?

No.

Had you knowledge of the indicator in the Control Room?

Yes, I noticed it working.

Had you seen it stopped at the dinner hour?

It was switched off during the lunch hour and when I went into the Control Room after lunch.

You saw it switched on afterwards?

Yes.

<u>By the President</u> - **Can you account for the statement made by Lieutenant Rideal that the vent indicator light was flickering?**

I can submit two possible reasons, (1) that the lamps or lamp holders were faulty, and (2) that the vents were not quite closed and were barely making contact on the indicating switches.

We have divers' evidence that all four vents were wide open, so that the only explanation possible in your opinion is the first one you gave to account for this flickering?

I am not aware of the conditions under which the flickering took place.

By Captain Hall - **We have had it in evidence that when Lieutenant Lane stated that the Boiler Room vents were shut the indicator was joined up the wrong way and that this indicating lamp was flickering; can you account for that in view of the fact that the vents were afterwards found wide open?**

No, I cannot account for it.

Otherwise than by the shaking-up movement?

That is possibly the case, but it is very unlikely in my opinion, I examined those lamps.

But the light was flickering and it showed that they were open?

I am unable to submit any explanation.

Except for the shaking up?

That always remains possible.

Is there any other evidence?

I can suggest none.

An indicating lamp, if it is correct, shows immediately the vent starts to open?

Yes, within the first quarter-inch movement.

PERCY A. HILLHOUSE

Called and Cautioned -

By the President - **We understand that you have no knowledge of the cause of this accident, but we would like to know if you have any remarks to offer about it or as to the conduct of operations afterwards by the people in the boat?**

Well, when it was seen that something was wrong there was a little excitement and orders were given out very rapidly indeed, but there was no panic of any kind, and nobody seemed to lose his head so far as I could see. The orders were given quickly and correctly and immediately carried out. All that was done or could be done was done immediately.

Subsequent to the captain's departure from the submarine?

Subsequent to his departure all that could be done for some considerable time was starting to pump at intervals, and in about half an hour the order was given to keep down the water, and after that we got a supply of compressed air it was necessary to blow out certain tanks, and that was carried out by Mr Searle and members of our own staff, Mr Bullen and Mr McLean.

I gather that Mr M'Lean and Mr Bullen and Mr Searle were leading hands?

Yes, assisted by members of the crew. They asked them to take up their stations and stand by the valves and they practically conducted operations.

<u>By Captain Hall</u> - **Was there bad air?**

Lieutenant Singer appeared to be suffering from severe pain and very severe headache.

Have you any remarks from a naval architect's point of view?

I do not think so. The accident, from what I have heard, was quite simple in its causes and results, and I do not think there is anything that may be learned from it except some sort of automatic signalling to show that these doors are closed. It is not automatic. That signal does not depend upon the movement of the valves themselves. Had there been some interlocking so that that signal could not have been set unless the valves were closed it would have been better.

Do you consider that under certain conditions the safety of the boat depends upon the whole of the operations being carried out practically simultaneously and if there is any defect in the automatic signalling arrangement you would lose the boat from the fact of her not having dived - do you think that would lead you to rely on the human element?

That is a practical point for consideration.

Have you any suggestion in connection with the general arrangements for safety that you can think of?

No.

Is there any outstanding point that struck you?

No, but there are a number of things, such as some means of renewing the oxygen or supplying helmets to escape by, had we not been able to raise the bows there was no means of our getting out at all.

The evidence was then closed, and after consideration the following judgment was drafted in a letter to Captain and Superintendent Barttelot, Clyde District:

Fairfield S. & E. Company,
19th February, 1917

Sir,

We have the honour to report that in compliance with your Memo, of 15 February 1917 we have this day held a full and careful investigation into the cause of the accident to H.M. Submarine K13, and the subsequent foundering in the Gare Loch. It would appear from the evidence that:

(a) The foundering was solely due to boiler intakes being open.

(b) The electric indicator showed that the intakes were open.

(c) Engineer-Lieutenant Lane believed the intakes closed.

(d) There is no foundation to support this belief of Lieutenant Lane.

It is possible that Lieutenant Rideal was mistaken in supposing that Lieutenant Lane was referring to intake indicators but there seems no doubt that he believed the boiler room intakes to be closed and that he reported his department shut off for diving.

The evidence clearly shows that the intake indicators had been working correctly and there is no reason to suppose that they did not do so on the last occasion.

161

We are therefore of the opinion that Engineer-Lieutenant Lane was solely responsible for the accident.

We consider that Lieutenant Commander Herbert was fully justified in believing that the submarine was all shut off for diving, but we would suggest that as a check on the electric indicator it would seem desirable to make use of the voice pipe also.

In conclusion we suggest that the names of Mr Frederick A Searle, Admiralty Overseer, Mr William McLean, Mr E. J. Skinner, and Mr F. Bullen, Managers at Fairfield, be submitted to their Lordships for commendation on account of their able services, which undoubtedly contributed materially towards the saving of the survivors.

The Court then rose.

No. 704/456

Sir,

I have the honour to report that the bodies of the officers and men who lost their lives in Submarine K13 were removed from the vessel during Thursday 15th March and Friday forenoon and buried at Shandon on Friday afternoon March 16th.

Only 29 bodies were recovered, 10 of which could not be identified. There are therefore 2 bodies not accounted for, and it appears possible that they are those of Engineer Lieutenant Lane and of Mr. Steel, senior engineer of the Fairfield company. This is only a supposition and cannot be definitely accepted in view of fact that 10 bodies were not recognisable.

The evidence in favour of the assumption is that

(1)   Eng. Lieutenant Lane was last seen in the engine room.

(2)   Mr. Steel was, in all probability, also in the engine room (where he was seen just before the accident).

(3)   No bodies were found in the engine room, but Eng. Lieut Lane's coat was found there.

(4)   The clips of the engine room hatch were open. . It is therefore possible that the two attempted to escape through the engine room

163

CHAPTER 4

THE BOARD OF INQUIRY REVISITED

A review of the minutes of the Board of Inquiry seem to show that the Board avoided any reference to the possibility of equipment failure or whether or not the submarine was correctly closed up and ready to dive. Instead they seem to have solely focused on the fact that it was human error that caused the accident. The conclusions reached by the Board are at best suspect, they appear to be anomalies in the statements given to the Board, some of which were contradictory and inconsistent.

The Inquiry was held only 14 days after the crew were rescued and almost four weeks before the submarine was raised and Admiralty Overseers and Fairfield engineers could actually inspect the submarine and determine valve and indicator positions. They relied on the testimony of four Royal Navy and six civilian witnesses, no independent expert witnesses were called. The Board sat for only a few hours before reaching its conclusions. Considering the circumstances and the loss of life, this seems a ludicrously short period of time.

More importantly, in a memo, dated 9 February 1917, Commodore S S Hall suggested 'that as some evidence may be required from Fairfield's employees, it would be most convenient if this were held at Govan *after the vessel is raised'*. (Author's italics). He continued that 'Departmental action has been taken as to informing "FEARLESS" and all "K" class to prevent a recurrence of this accident, by having a check on error of a human element'. It seems that the Commodore had already decided what caused the accident and perhaps the Board's main purpose was to substantiate his view.

There are a number of points that should be kept in mind before re-examining the Board's minutes. First it should be remembered that the language is a hundred years old, it seems more formal and perhaps not as precise as you might expect from a current enquiry or investigation. The manner in which the Navy seems to have gone about its business seems odd, especially to the modern submariner such as announcing Diving Stations over lunch. Also, the idea of diving a submarine to look for a leak might seem alien, if not positively dangerous to the modern submariner. Although in the days before the vacuum test, boats would 'dip' under the water to check watertight integrity. Any thoughts of checkoff lists, Books of Reference (BRs), Operating Instructions or quality assurance systems should be laid aside. Tasks were learned on site, it was very much a hands-on learning environment. The accident wasn't reported at the time due to the wartime news blackout.

It would not be unreasonable to question the suitability of the Board members to sit in judgement of this accident, after all it was the Navy's newest submarine, new technology and the accident was responsible for a great loss of life.

Acting Captain Godfrey A. Corbett, RN
President

Born 1 July 1871, he was promoted Lieutenant in November 1892. In mid-1905, Corbett was thanked for inventing a "submarine kite", though it was not accepted for use. He was promoted to the rank of Commander on 30 June, 1906. Corbett was appointed in command of a ship, and as Flag Commander, on 7 January, 1911 until 11 April, 1911. In February 1913, he was blamed for damage that Melpomene incurred while being undocked. He was promoted to the rank of Acting Captain on 3 July, 1915.

Commander Aubrey T. Tillard, K.B.E., D.S.O.
Firedrake

He was promoted to the rank of Lieutenant on 31 March, 1903 then appointed in command of the destroyer Larne on 28 January, 1911. He was promoted to the rank of Lieutenant-Commander on 31 March, 1911. He was promoted to the rank of Commander on 31 December, 1914. He commanded the destroyer HMS Firedrake in 1917. During his career he held a considerable number of seagoing appointments.

Commander Ferdinand E.B. Feilman
H.M. Submarine K 14

He was born in Calcutta, India on 19th August 1883 and joined the Royal Navy as a Cadet at HMS BRITANNIA on 15th January 1898.

During his long Naval career, he acquired a great deal of experience in submarines. After several appointments he joined the Submarine Depot Ship HMS THAMES for training, on 5 April 1904. He was promoted Lieutenant on 1 April 1905 and on 18 June 1905 he was re-appointed to HMS THAMES in command of submarine C1. He returned to General Service on 25 August 1908.

Two years later he was appointed to the Submarine Depot Ship HMS VULCAN in command of submarine C39. He was re-appointed to the Submarine Depot Ship HMS THAMES in command of C1. This appointment lasted until November 1911 when he returned to General Service. His next Submarine appointment was to HMS ARROGANT, the Depot Ship of the Fourth Submarine Flotilla at Portsmouth, where he commanded C16. He then commanded E7 while it was building at Chatham. His next appointment was to the Submarine Depot Ship HMS ARROGANT (4th Submarine Flotilla) at Dover where he commanded C2. This was followed by his third Wartime Command, E31, which was building at Scott's of Greenock.

He was promoted to Commander on 31 December 1916 and, on 15 February 1917, was appointed to K14 which was building at Fairfield.

Commodore Captain Sydney Hall,
Admiralty Adviser

The third Inspecting Captain of Submarines. He was primarily a technician, an inventor and a torpedo man, who thoroughly understood the workings and complexities of the submarine. He designed the first submarine escape helmet and the D-class submarine gun mounting.

He predicted that submarines could be used to torpedo merchant ships and by 1920 was forecasting the rise of air power. Very controversially he stated this would lead to the battleship becoming obsolete. Arguably this refusal to 'toe the Company line' made him an ideal candidate to lead the fledgling submarine branch.

He had been confirmed in the rank of Sub-Lieutenant, 14 August, 1891 and subsequently promoted to Lieutenant 14 August, 1892. In July 1901 he was appointed to command TB 81, HMS Swift and was placed in command of the Portsmouth Flotilla for the annual manoeuvres. Unfortunately, this was not a particularly successful appointment, he stranded T.B. 81 at Alderney on a submerged breakwater on 1 August. The damage was so bad that she sank and had to be salvaged. The subsequent Court of Inquiry found that the sinking had been "caused by great carelessness on [Hall's] part" and they expressed their "extreme displease" at his actions. They, perhaps not unexpectedly, advised that he should be more careful in future. Despite this he was promoted Commander on 1 January, 1903, and three years later appointed in command of the submarine depot ship Mercury and as Inspecting Commander of Submarines. He was promoted Captain on 31 December, 1907. On 4 February 1911, he was appointed in command of the second class protected cruiser Diana. Then after a spell as Joint Secretary of the Oil Fuel Commission, he was appointed to command the armoured cruiser Roxburgh in July, 1914.

When Lord Fisher became First Sea Lord in October 1914, he appointed Hall on 31 October as an Additional Naval Assistant for Submarine Duties. He became the Royal Navy's top submarine

officer, as Commodore (S) on 8 February, 1915. Although his office was at the Admiralty, he was also captain of HMS Dolphin from 8 February, 1915. He
While he was ICS, he constantly stressed the importance of the crew, he also supported a policy of continuous submarine evolution and emphasised the value of large classes of identical vessels. His belief that the crew was promoted Commodore, First Class on 1 January, 1918.

were more important than the submarine and his emphasis on training resulted in British submariners, probably, being the most proficient in the world.

The four Board members were senior experienced Naval Officers. All had command experience, Commander Ferdinand E.B. Feilman had captained several submarines. Despite this I consider the Board's findings, at best flawed and re-examination of the Board's minutes shows serious oversights and errors of judgement.

A re-examination of the Minutes

Significant points arising from the minutes are considered below. As in Chapter 3, the Boards questions are in Bold, the 'interviewees' responses are in normal type. The exchanges have been reproduced in full, so readers will not have to flip backwards and forwards. The author's comments are in italics, at the end of each exchange.

Lt Cdr Herbert

By Captain Hall - **When was the order given to "diving stations" before you turned the boat up?**

Some minutes before.

How was the order passed on?

Down the Control Room and down the Engine Room hatch by myself. I was on the top of the super-structure and I gave the order down the Engine Room hatch. I asked a stoker why he was not at his diving station, and I sent him back.

Herbert was on the casing, there is every chance he could see the intakes. He knew there was an unexplained leak, would it not be prudent to check the covers and funnels?

Did you give any orders during the dinner hour as to the opening up of the Boiler Room?

Yes.

What were they?

I told the Engine Room attendant in charge to do what he wanted to ventilate the Boiler Room.

Referring to Lt Lane as the Engine Room Attendant is dismissive and shows how engineers were viewed. Lt Lane was only one rank below Lt Cdr Herbert.

By the President - **Why do you state in your report that the First Lieutenant reported that the Engine Room was shut off?**

Because I was on deck and he was in the Control Room, and it is customary to receive a report from him before coming down from the Conning Tower. On an occasion like this when there was no hurry - I want to say that it was different from a service dive in this way that it was in slow time. I waited till I saw everything, as far as I could see, shut down and the funnels themselves shut up.

The intakes were fully open, as noted above, he could have seen them.

When you came down would you be able to see whether the indicator was as he reported?

Yes, it was a red light from a conspicuous place in the middle of the room and you cannot mistake it.

A red light indicating that it was shut off?

Yes, it is enclosed in a screen in the Engine Room and "shut off" engraved on it.

Presumably the Captain was referring to the Control Indicator that showed the Boiler Room was shut off.

<u>By the President</u> – **Even if he were in the Boiler Room could he readily see the indicator?**

Not without climbing up on the top of the grating.

<u>By Captain Hall</u> - **Is there not a special indicator for the express purpose of showing that?**

It is not down on the platform at the furnace doors.

But it is in full view of the Stoker-Hold?

Yes.

Seems confusing, there must be a mechanical indicator directly connected to the intakes.

<u>By Commander Feilman</u> - **Had they plenty of time in the Boiler Room before you prepared to dive after you gave the order "diving stations"?**

Yes - ample time - five or six minutes.

One must ask if this really is an adequate amount of time. Although the boilers were shut down there were still several tasks to be completed, the record for diving a K boat was some 23 minutes.

<u>By Commander Feilman</u> - **Could you easily see whether the vents were closed?**

Quite easily.

Was this a reference to the Control Room indicator or the actual vents?

And you dived specially for that purpose?

Yes, especially to see if these vents were tight.

Again, this is a very important point. Cdr Herbert would have been able to see the state of the vents. Surely he would check, after all, this was the whole purpose of the dive.

Are you quite sure that it was shut off during the dinner hour?

I am not certain myself, but I know somebody who saw it off.

Not very factual. Why didn't the Board ask who this was? And did this person pass on the message.

Does he receive a report in addition to the second Petty Officer in the Boiler Room?

Presumably, yes. I had not given him instructions. Very often you cannot stay in the Boiler Room when it is shut off and everyone quits the Boiler Room at once.

This is speculation.

LIEUT. PARIS G. SINGER, K13.

Can you give us a general account of what happened? –

I came over from the "Comet" and there was an order "diving stations". The funnels were being turned down just then, and I sang out to tell them to delay. They were just going to dive. Someone waved his hand and went down the Engine Room hatch. I went down through the Conning Tower into the Control Room and saw all the necessary hydroplanes and motors running, and as soon as everything was ready for diving, I saw that the lights in the indicating room were shut off. I reported to the Captain, and I forget exactly the orders that were given. When the Captain came down he asked if the Engine Room was shut off, and I reported to him that it was. The lights were turned on again and he gave the order to flood externals, and then in a minute or two minutes to dive to twenty feet. The first time I noticed anything wrong was the pressure of air in the ears, and at the same time I was standing near the voice pipe and I heard through the voice pipe "surface, Boiler Room flooded". I sang out, I forget the exact words, but I said "surface, Boiler Room flooded". I do not remember the exact sequence of two or three orders. Then I heard "close water-tight doors", and I immediately saw that the air was in the tanks. I went back to see that the water-tight doors were being closed. I also gave the order to drop the keel forward. I went back to the water-tight doors in the after-Control Room, and one of the indicators was the wrong way, and it would not shut. It was just then that the main motor fuses blew. The door was shut and I went forward to see that the keel was dropped. I think that was all.

Why did he tell them to delay, were they securing the funnels? Why wasn't this explored by the Board?

One of the indicators on the water tight doors at the aft of Control Room was the wrong way. Is this significant, perhaps it was indicative of a build fault? Why did the Board not pursue this?

Did the water come in all the time that you were down there?

No, sir, by that time we had a list to port and 40 degrees up from the bow.

Should be 4, probably a typing error. It is surprising it was not corrected when it was proof read.

<u>By Captain Hall</u> - **When you got the orders "diving stations" did you get them direct from the Captain?**

No, they were given when I was at lunch.

Do you know how they were passed over?

It should have been by voice pipe.
Should have been? Didn't it happen like that?

You were not down below when the orders "diving stations" were given?

No.

Had you any personal knowledge of the procedure adopted at the after part of the vessel when "diving stations" were ordered?

In the Engine Room?

Yes?

I knew that it had to be shut off.

Had you laid down the stations?

Yes.

This whole exchange seems a little confusing. Diving stations orders passed over at the lunch table. Knowing the Engine Room had to be shut off seems a little simplistic.

LIEUTENANT (E) LEONARD C. RIDEAL, K14

By the President - **Will you state to the Court what happened from the time the order was given to dive up to the time when you arrived in the Control Room?**

I did not hear the order to dive at all. I came down through the Control Room and went into the Engine Room and Lieutenant Lane was working the funnel operating gear. He finished that and then I went over to the Boiler Room vent indicator on the port side. I noticed the lower one. The lower light was flickering and it looked to be showing the vent opening. I asked Lieutenant Lane about that and he said it had been connected up the wrong way round, and nothing further was done. He then gave the order to close down the Engine Room hatch. I did not see that done because I was looking forward at the time and he sent the Chief E.R.A. to see if they were making any water. The Chief E.R.A. came back almost at once and reported that there was a good deal coming in and he closed the door after him. As soon as the Chief E.R.A. had come out of the Boiler Room I saw the water coming through the exhaust pump which leads through into the Boiler Room, and Lieutenant Lane was at the starboard one. I then decided to come through and tell the Captain what was happening. As I was coming through into the Control Room Lieutenant Singer was just closing the door into the Control Room, and I reported to Commander Goodhart what had happened in the Engine Room.

Mentions the flickering light, why didn't he ask Lt Lane to clarify his answer. Why would Lt Lane say this? He heard the order to shut the Engine room hatch. It seems a little strange that he reported to Commander Goodhart and not the actual boat's captain?

177

By the President - **What made you ask the question about the vents being closed or not?**

Because I saw the light flickering and knew that Lieutenant Lane was about to dive and I knew that the vents were being closed. I was not aware that he had dived.

He states he was aware the vents were being closed, why didn't he say more and question Lt Lane further. He must have been aware of the consequences if the submarine dived with the intakes open.

When you were in the Engine Room alongside the Engine Room Lieutenant of the ship, did you know that preparations to dive were being made?

Yes, I did.

Did you hear any report made to the Engine Room Lieutenant from the Boiler Room that the Boiler Room was shut off for diving?

No.

Did you not expect to hear one in view of your doubts about the vents?

I had my doubts about the vents and that was what made me speak to Lieutenant Lane about them.

Were you quite satisfied with his reply?

I thought it rather unusual.

This should have been explored further, why would Lt Lane make up an answer or tell a lie. He was a competent and capable

178

officer. Somebody must have brief him on this, he wouldn't have made this up. .

Was there any light showing in the lamp to indicate "Vents closed"?

I do not remember any other light except the lower of the two lights which certainly was flickering "Vents open" and that was the one that attracted my attention. The others in the room were right, but I saw the lower one flickering, indicating "Vents open".

An assumption that a flickering light meant the vents were opening, why did Lt Riddell think this? Why didn't he act upon this, he was more than well aware of the consequences.

The other lamp was not showing anything?

I would not make any statement about the other lamp. These lights are about 8 inches apart.

By Captain Hall - **Was there any possibility of your mistaking the thing being open or shut by these lamps?**

If they are connected up the wrong way.

But if they are working correctly?

Reading "Vents open" or "Vents closed". I do not remember whether the upper light was burning or not. I would not make any statement about the upper light.

Were you in the Engine Room or Boiler Room after dinner?

No, I came out as soon as it was over.

Confusing exchange, the Board should have asked for further clarification.

You saw these lights flickering when they were shutting off for diving?

Yes.

And you pointed that out to Lieutenant Lane?

Yes.

Did he do anything about it or go to the Boiler Room to see?

I did not notice him doing anything. He was apparently satisfied that the vents were closed because he told me that 'they had' been connected up the wrong way round.

Why didn't he ask more questions and why would Lt Lane say they were wired up the wrong way?

Was there any water in the Engine Room when you left it other than that coming through the ventilator?

I could not be sure, I thought that it was coming through the ventilator.

He said he saw water coming through the exhaust pump.

FREDERICK WILLIAM SEARLE.

Do you know of your own knowledge that this gear was all right on the day that it was being worked?

Yes. I knew for a fact that Lieutenant Lane spoke to me about these ventilators and he asked me if I would come and have a look at them. He said that he thought one ventilator was slightly sticking when being opened.

Was this after dinner?

No, this was in the morning and I came on deck with him and the port after ventilator was about three-quarters of an inch up and not fully at the stops, and since I was able to explain why that would happen I did not worry.

How could you tell they were working?

Because they must be open or shut and Lieutenant Lane had told me that he had worked them and this little one was not fully opened. I knew exactly what had happened but after that it was proved conclusively that the four could be opened hard on the stops. They were there at lunch time between the first and second dives.

How do you know?

Lieutenant Lane came into the Boiler Room, but I am not a good witness for this. During the lunch hour Lieutenant Lane had opened these vents to cool the Boiler Room as much as possible, so that really what we intended diving for in the afternoon was a leak and he wanted to cool the Boiler Room, and he sent his Chief E.R.A. to see whether these vents were wide open then. I did not hear the E.R.A come back.

It is difficult to understand why the Board did not ask him to explain this. It should have been explored further.

Do you consider it possible for the Boiler Room vent handle to be worked with the stop valve shut, so that the officer would think that he had been closing the Boiler Room vents when in reality nothing was happening?

Yes, I do think it is possible. I myself have often worked the handles of these vents when there has been no pressure and I thought that there was pressure, and I had to go back and slacken the pressure. There is one invariable way of telling, there is a

181

pressure gauge. Every time you work the handle you can see it taking up the pressure and anyone can make the handle go back again.

Was that pointed out to the crew?

Yes, to my knowledge. It was absolutely pointed out to the men in the Control Room who work the whole of these vents.

The vents were not controlled from Control Room, this should have been challenged by the Board and surely the Board should have had the knowledge to question this.

WILLIAM M'LEAN, Submarine Manager at Fairfield.

Did you notice during the dinner hour that the light showing that it had been closed was burning, or not?

No, I did not notice it. I looked at it, and it was burning then.

Confusing, if it was showing closed, the intakes were open during the lunch hour. Was this indicator working at all. Presumably this is referring to the Control Room indicator.

EDWARD J. SKINNER, Manager of Fairfield Electrical Department.

Called and Cautioned -

By Captain Hall -
Is it possible that they could have been joined up the wrong way?

No, practically impossible.

You cannot think of what gave rise for anyone saying that they were turned the wrong way?

182

No, and there was nothing reported to me as being wrong.

Did it come out from evidence that they were joined up the wrong way?

Yes, if the doors went close, they would not shut correctly.

Does not that show that they were open?

Yes, there was a light showing that these doors were open.

This is a confusing exchange, was he referring to the vents, funnels, what doors? What was the 'evidence', seeing that at this time the submarine was still at the bottom of the Gare Loch. More importantly, this seems to validate Lt Lane's version of events. As mentioned above, the Control Door seems to have been wired up the wrong way.

Can you account for the Boiler Room electrical indicator flickering?

No.

The fact that they were wired up wrong perhaps.

WILLIAM STRUTHERS

<u>By the President</u> - **Will you tell the Court what you know of what happened from the time the order was given to dive or to prepare for diving?**

When I went on board about half-past 3 I was in the Control Room, and they had not started to dive and I was not there when the order was given to dive, but I was in the Control Room when the order "diving stations" was given. I knew that the order had been given. I only heard another order when I was in the Control Room by-Lieut. Singer, which was to open all externals. I then went aft to the Turbine Room, and while I was in the Turbine Room I spoke in the Engine Room to Lieutenant Lane, and I also saw him operating the after funnel gear that is on the starboard side of the ship. Shortly after that he said that he did not know whether the Boiler Room vents were closed or not. Shortly after that I asked the E.R.A. who was responsible for the Boiler Room vents, if he had closed the vents and he assured me that he had. I expect that by that time we were diving, because I know that the motor was going. I assumed that we were diving. Lieutenant Lane sent his Chief E.R.A. into the Boiler Room to see how things were and the Chief E.R.A. opened the Boiler Room door and closed it behind him. He was only gone five or six seconds when he returned and said that the Boiler Room was flooding freely. He closed the door behind him and clipped off the door. Lieutenant Lane then said to the man at the voice pipe to tell the skipper to come to the surface immediately as the Boiler Room was flooding fast. Just immediately after that I went forward through the passage to get to the Control Room and there was water coming into the passage when I went through. There were some glands in the after end of the funnel clip gear and I also looked into the bull's eye in the passage and could see that the water was flooding up past there. I got to the other end of the Boiler Room passage between the Torpedo Room and the Turbine Room and one of the service men, I think a reserve man - was stationed at the foot of the ladder and was closing the door at the time. I got through there and got to the Control Room door which was closed. I turned back, and I think it was a torpedo man in the Beam Room who was attending to the door and he shut it behind me. I got into the Control Room, but the water was coming out of the voice pipes. The Captain then asked me if I could get pushed up to the top and turn the voice pipe cock off. (I said that the water was putting out the fires and they were blowing the tanks

Lt Lane seems to say he didn't know if the vents were shut. This is unbelievable. Lane asked for the dive to check the vents, he would have known if they were open or closed.

184

Was this after you came on board the submarine?

No. The first time was on the "Comet" and it was when we were on the deck of the "Comet" that he asked the E.R.A. to see. The "Comet" was lying alongside. While I was in the Turbine Room, I spoke to him and also the assistant overseer, and I intended to go into the Boiler Room and see if there were any leaks. We were talking about things in general when he said that he did not know whether they were open or not. It seemed as if he were speaking his thoughts aloud. I did not think any more about it at the time, but the place where the vents were was a little congested and there were two or three men there, and I was at the opposite corner. The artificer who was responsible for the job had spoken to me two or three times about operating this trial, and I asked him casually when passing if he had closed the vents, and he said he had, and I did not think any more of it at the time.

Seems to be blaming the Navy.

Do you think that he would be likely to operate the lever without opening the stop valve?

I cannot say that he was likely to do it, but that is a thing that might happen with any party, locking them by the opening valve and perhaps forgetting just for an instant in closing the vents.

Leading question

By Captain Hall - **What did you say to Lieut. Lane when you first went into the Turbine Room?**

I had been speaking to him at lunch on board the "Comet", and he told me that he had arranged with the Captain to have another short dive. While on board the "Comet" after lunch we came up on deck and Lieutenant Lane was particularly interested in the

Boiler Room vents. He called up to his Chief E.R.A. to go and see what position they were in. The Chief E.R.A. was aft and the Chief Stoker went up on the superstructure and he said that they were full open. Lieutenant Lane was quite pleased with that and that was all right.

Any reason why he asked the ERA about the vents. Lt Lane is interested in the vents, they were upmost in his mind, surely he would have ensured they were shut?

Is this after you came on board the submarine?

No. The first time was on the "Comet" and it was when we were on the deck of the "Comet" that he asked the E.R.A. to see. The "Comet" was lying alongside. While I was in the Turbine Room, I spoke to him and also the assistant overseer, and I intended to go into the Boiler Room and see if there were any leaks. We were talking about things in general when he said that he did not know whether they were open or not. It seemed as if he were speaking his thoughts aloud. I did not think any more about it at the time, but the place where the vents were was a little congested and there were two or three men there, and I was at the opposite corner. The artificer who was responsible for the job had spoken to me two or three times about operating this trial, and I asked him casually when passing if he had closed the vents, and he said he had, and I did not think any more of it at the time.

It is hard to believe that Lt Lane didn't know the state of the vents, unless he was expressing a genuine concern with the indicators. It seems strange that Mr Struthers, after hearing Lt. Lane's reply, didn't think any more about it at the time or pursue the matter further.

WILLIAM HANCOCK, Admiralty Electrical Overseer

By Captain Hall -

Had you knowledge of the indicator in the Control Room?

Yes, I noticed it working.

Had you seen it stopped at the dinner hour?

It was switched off during the lunch hour and when I went into the Control Room after lunch.

You saw it switched on afterwards?

Yes.

Maybe it was still showing the mornings shut off for diving and had not been reset.

By the President - **Can you account for the statement made by Lieutenant Rideal that the vent indicator light was flickering?**
—

I can submit two possible reasons, (1) that the lamps or lamp holders were faulty, and (2) that the vents were not quite closed and were barely making contact on the indicating switches.

We have divers' evidence that all four vents were wide open, so that the only explanation possible in your opinion is the first one you gave to account for this flickering?

I am not aware of the conditions under which the flickering took place.

The Board are saying the lamp is faulty, surely the second reason is valid.

By Captain Hall - **We have had it in evidence that when Lieutenant Lane stated that the Boiler Room vents were shut the indicator was joined up the wrong way and that this**

187

indicating lamp was flickering; can you account for that in view of the fact that the vents were afterwards found wide open?

No, I cannot account for it.

Otherwise than by the shaking-up movement?

That is possibly the case, but it is very unlikely in my opinion, I examined those lamps.

But the light was flickering and it showed that they were open?

I am unable to submit any explanation.

This all seems very confusing. Why didn't the Board seek clarification?

Except for the shaking up?

That always remains possible.

Is there any other evidence?

I can suggest none.

An indicating lamp, if it is correct, shows immediately the vent starts to open?

Yes, within the first quarter-inch movement.

Discussion

As pointed out above there were many inconsistencies in the Board's questioning and in the answers they received. Also, for

188

whatever reason, many seemingly important points were not pursued. They only seemed to consider that the accident was a result of personal fault from the very outset and never examined the possibility of equipment failure. This is particularly noticeable in the fact that the Board failed to further explore Mr Searle's remarks about the intakes not closing correctly or the rather confusing exchange with Mr Skinner about the indicator light wiring.

They never sought the opinion of independent technical experts and it must be remembered that the prime exhibit, the submarine itself, was still under the water, the exhibit that contained all the answers. Commodore S S Hall suggested in his memo that the Board should be held after the submarine was raised. He also stated that the necessary action had been taken to inform all K-class submarines and their depot ships of the measures required to prevent an accident of this type happening again. It advised that checks should be put in place to ensure that any chance of human error was eliminated. The Commodore was the Board's technical expert, yet he seemed to have a preconceived notion of what caused the submarine to sink and that certainly didn't seem to include any consideration of mechanical failure. Understandably the Navy wanted this episode settled and perhaps ICS wanted to see his memo confirmed.

There are two major issues that the Board didn't address adequately:

Firstly, undoubtedly, is what caused the sudden and catastrophic flooding of the stern compartments. The submarine didn't sink because the Boiler Room flooded. The submarine sank because the water, somehow, escaped from the Boiler Room.
Arguably this is the most important point, how did the water get out of the Boiler Room and so quickly? The Board didn't look at this at all. In his War Diary, Cox'n Moth states that the Boiler Room 'door' blew open. Maybe he had heard this when he re-joined the salvaged K13, K22.

Secondly, they didn't satisfactorily explain the flicker indicator light. They were working in the morning and several Fairfield employees testified that the lights were working correctly. What happened over the lunch period to cause the flickering, surely this should have been investigated?

Apart from these two points and anomalies in the Board's minutes, several other major issues do not seem to have been considered or pursued at all by the Board:

1. Herbert accepted the submarine, on behalf of the Navy, with an unexplained defect.

2. Nobody mentioned the switchboard fire caused by the water 'spurting' out of the voice pipe. Important for compiling a timeline.

3. The source of the 200 gallons of water in the Boiler Room, the precursor to the final dive, was not explored.

4. The previous history of the submarine, for example the damage to the funnel during trials, the sinking in the Fairfield yard and the grounding were not explored

5. Lt Lane queried the operation of the air intakes, what was the Admiralty Overseers explanation?

6. Why weren't the air bottles topped up during the lunch break?

7. Why did the Admiralty Supervisor specifically ask the ERA about the intakes? Seems strange, why not the funnels etc.

8. Why didn't the Board question the number of people on Board, this increased weight by approximately 40%. This would have reduced the reserve buoyancy.

9. The Board didn't seem interested in compiling a timeline of events.

10. No other K boats accidents were mentioned or used as reference, the Board didn't seem to think that other K-class accidents were relevant.

Despite these apparent short comings, using the very limited and questionable evidence as well as numerous assumptions available to them, the Board concluded:

(a) The foundering was solely due to boiler intakes being open.
(b) The electric indicator showed that the intakes were open.
(c) Engineer-Lieutenant Lane believed the intakes closed.
(d) There is no foundation to support this belief of Lieutenant Lane.

They felt it was possible that Lieutenant Rideal was mistaken in supposing that Lieutenant Lane was referring to intake indicators, but there seemed no doubt that Lt Lane believed the Boiler Room intakes were closed and that he reported his department shut off for diving.

They were therefore of the opinion that Engineer-Lieutenant Lane was solely responsible for the accident, they considered that Lieutenant Commander Herbert was fully justified in believing that the submarine was shut off for diving. They suggested that, as well as checking on the electric indicator, it would be desirable to make use of the voice pipe.

In view of the points raised above, the Board's findings can be viewed in a somewhat different light:
The foundering was solely due to boiler intakes being open.

Questionable point and not strictly true. The Boiler Room flooding would probably have not resulted in sinking the submarine, despite it being overweight due to the number of people on board. The boat sank because the Boiler Room / Engine Room bulkhead failed and as a result of this, all the back aft compartments were flooded.

This is pivotal, the flooded aft compartments caused the sinking. This may have been a build fault but it could not be confirmed because the boat was still under the water.

If the aft compartments hadn't flooded, the crew could have blown tanks, released the drop keel etc. Why the Board didn't pursue this line of enquiry is open to conjecture, they simply may have thought it was not an important or relevant point. Whether or not the bulkhead failed, the water unquestionably entered the submarine via the Boiler Room vents.

The electric indicator showed that the intakes were open.

The indicator light didn't show the intakes were open, it was flickering. Several Fairfield employees testified to the Board that they were working, they were certainly working on the previous dive. The flickering light must have shown that the intakes moved, someone had actually operated the valve. The Boards failure to recognise this must be its major failing.

Engineer-Lieutenant Lane believed the intakes closed.

He did and with good reason. The ERA, who was responsible for closing the air intakes, confirmed he had shut them. Mr Struthers mentions talking to the ERA, he asked him if he closed the intakes, and he said he had. Even if he hadn't, surely it would prod his memory and he would scuttle away and correct his oversight. He must have been aware of the consequences of diving with the intakes open. Nobody is more aware of the dangers a submariner faces than the submariner himself.

The second dive was at the request of Lt Lane. Would he not ensure that the intakes were closed? They were a potential source of the water in the Boiler Room.

There is no foundation to support this belief of Lieutenant Lane (that the intakes were shut)

There certainly was evidence to support Lt Lane's conviction, the ERA confirmed he had shut the intakes.

Yet despite this, the Board concluded that Engineer-Lieutenant Lane was solely responsible for the accident. The Board were not required to justify or record their reasoning for reaching this decision. Very strong words, a damming indictment that was guaranteed to ruin Lt Lane's reputation, especially as he was unable to defend himself. As a result of the verdict, his widowed wife was not entitled to a pension. Lt Lane's father had to intervene to ensure his daughter-in-law and granddaughter had a small pension.

Why would the Board reach this decision? Several people were in a position to see the position of the intakes before the dive, not least of whom was the Captain himself. The accident would undoubtedly be bad PR and affect the moral of serving submariners; the country was at war, a serious fault on its newest submarine would be encouraging news for the enemy. It was certainly in Fairfield's and the Navy's interest that they were not blamed. Of course from the evidence available to them, the board could have truly believed Lt Lane was responsible, however, whether the Board should have reached the verdict they did with the evidence provided to them is another matter.

CHAPTER 5

AN ALTERNATIVE SCENARIO

At the end of January 1917, the recently completed submarine K2 sailed from Portsmouth on acceptance trials. That day the sea was choppy and the temperature was freezing, ice was forming on the shore. Soon after the submarine left the shelter of the harbour, water began to slop into the casing beneath the funnels and through the mushroom shaped ventilators into the boiler-room. In Stokes Bay the submarine prepared to dive and the vents opened to flood the main ballast tanks. In the Engine Room an ERA operated the lever to close the Boiler Room vents but the electrical indicator did not light up. The Engineer Officer, Alexander Mark-Wardlaw, shouted down the voice-pipe to the Control-Room: 'Surface immediately!' Fortunately, the call came in time and the submarine surfaced. Mark-Wardlaw examined the vents and concluded that the icy sea-water had partly solidified the oil in the hydraulic system. Wax must have settled out of the oil, jamming the actuating cylinders. Back in harbour, as he took a sample of oil to the Admiralty chemists to test his theory, news came through of the sinking of K13 in the Gare Loch. The chemist confirmed that the oil from K2 was a type which became wax-bound at around 30°F. An instruction immediately went out to all K boats to use Arctic non-freezing oil in their hydraulic systems.

This incident casts the sinking of K13 in a whole new light and when the submarine sailed on that fateful morning, maybe the die was already cast and her eventual fate was no longer in the hands of her crew.

Admittedly, what follows is speculation and conjecture, I would argue that this is much the same as the original Board of Inquiry.

In keeping with many others of the class, K13's brief life was eventful and ultimately disastrous. Her keel was laid down 2 October 1916 and she was launched at 11 November 1916 by the wife of the submarine's Commanding Officer. The hydroplanes were damaged as the submarine ran down the slipway.

Following the repair, she conducted a basin dive, where she unexpectedly sank to the bottom. After this the submarine was moved to Govan Dry Dock for final painting where, due to a wrong valve line up, the engine and motor room were flooded. On 18 January1917, during the speed trials, she damaged her funnels in heavy seas.

She was due to leave the yard for her final acceptance trials at 0800 Monday 29 January 1917 but a problem with one of the mooring wires caused a delay. On board were 80 men; 53 RN crew, 14 employees of the Govan ship builder, 5 Admiralty officials, 5 other civilians, a pilot and the captain and engineer of sister submarine K14, which was also building at Fairfield, to gain K-boat experience.

A mile down the river she ran aground. Lt Cdr Herbert, K13's Commanding Officer, allowed the tide to bring the stern right around before going astern and proceeding backwards down the river. It was only when he reached a tributary, known as the Cart, that he had room to put her about.

K13 reached the Gare Loch at 11:30. She then carried out full power trials and other tests that were required as part of the acceptance programme; starting, stopping, full speed, turning, going astern. During this period the boilers were supplying the power. All of these trials were completed successfully.

During the trial dive, she remained submerged for approximately 2 hours. On surfacing, her Engineer, Lieutenant Arthur Lane, reported that a small leak in the Boiler Room had resulted in some 200 gallons of water entering the compartment.

The heat in the Boiler Room made it impossible for anyone to determine the source of the leak. He suggested a further short dive to determine the source of the leak and to check the water tightness of the funnel covers and Boiler Room ventilators. Despite this, Cdr Herbert accepted the submarine on behalf of the Royal Navy providing the submarine was dry docked to check for damage after the grounding.

During this dive there were no reports of flickering indicator lights.

Two Fairfield directors, Mr. Cleghorn and Mr. Macmillan, were put ashore. Mr. Macmillan had to make arrangements for the docking while the crew had lunch aboard the Comet, a small tender.

After lunch, the crew prepared the submarine for the test dive.

From the official weather reports of the day, the air temperature in the Gare Loch was 32°F (freezing point). While the Boiler Room was pumped out and ventilated, presumably the fans were used to draw air into the Boiler Room. This would have added a degree of wind chill. This is when the hydraulic oil waxed. It didn't happen in the morning because the Boiler Room was hot.

Air for the boilers entered the Boiler Room through four openings in the pressure hull, these were 37" in diameter. There were two turbo-fans directly below the intakes to draw air into the compartment. When dived, these intakes were covered by metal plates which prevented the seawater from flooding the Boiler Room. These were dome-shaped with lugs on their rims, which slid on vertical bars, they were raised about 10" by a hydraulic ram to allow air to enter. Each cover weighed about 8 cwts and this weight helped them close. Several systems were installed to operate the covers. In some designs a hydraulic ram pressed down on the cover to keep it on its seating when shut. On K13 the intakes were kept open by hydraulic pressure on the rams. When the pressure was removed, a spring and the weight of the covers forced the cover onto its seat. The covers could also be operated by hand in the event of a hydraulic failure.

Two turbo-fans were positioned directly below the air intakes to draw air into the Boiler Room.

The control valve for operating the funnels and air intakes was fitted in the Turbine Room, near the Boiler / Engine Room airlock hatch. This was a two-way block valve operated by a lever. Moving the lever to the open position allowed high pressure hydraulic oil to flow through two stop valves to two pressure regulating accumulators. The hydraulic pressure then operated two spring loaded slave cylinders which were mounted either side of each of the four ventilators. These eight cylinders operated simultaneously to open the four ventilators.

When the lever was moved to the Close position the hydraulic pressure collapsed, the fluid drained away and the four ventilators shut under spring tension aided by the weight of the covers themselves. Two pressure gauges gave an indication of the pressure in the high-pressure pipeline downstream of the block valve.

The submarine had a common hydraulic system which operated the funnel units and their hatch covers, Boiler Room ventilator domes, ventilation ports, periscope and radio masts raising and lowering. Two Hele Shaw pumps provided a system pressure of 1800 psi.

Normally when the submarine was preparing to dive, watch keepers had to leave the Boiler Room due to the heat. Electrical indicators were fitted in the Turbine Room to show the position of the intake covers. Mechanical indicators, showing whether the ventilators were open or closed, were positioned in the Boiler Room. These were directly connected to the intake covers.

The intake covers travel up and down on guide rods, and when they have travelled about a quarter of an inch to half an inch, from the open to the closed position, a contact is made and the indicator light changes from open to closed.

The flickering indicator light showed that the valve must have been put to the shut position or the indicator would have stayed showing open. Several Fairfield workers testified that the indicator lights were working correctly and they seemed to have done so a few hours previously during the first dive.

This time though, the intakes could not fully close, they were unable to move further because of the waxing, in the actuating cylinders. In fact, they could only move as far as the indicator contacts, which was about between a quarter to half an inch and then they jammed. As the indicator 'dithered' over the contacts, the intermittent contact caused the flickering of the indicator light.

This doesn't explain why Lt Lane would lie or make up a story about the lights being wired up wrongly nor does it clarify why he should say he didn't know the position of the vents.

Edward Skinner, the manager of the Electrical Department at Fairfield's, was asked by Captain Hall at the Board of Inquiry if it was possible that the indicator lights could have been joined up the wrong way. He replied it was practically impossible. He went on to say that he could not think of a reason why anybody, (Lt Lane) should say the lights were wired up the wrongly. He also stated that nobody had reported any faults with the indicator lights.

The next part of his evidence was very confusing and it is surprising that the Board didn't seek further clarification as it seems to have had the potential to influence their final decision. Mr. Skinner was asked, "Did it come out from evidence that they were joined up the wrong way?" He replied "Yes, if the doors went close, they would not shut correctly".

What this evidence was or how it was obtained is not addressed. It could not have come from an inspection of the submarine, as it was still at the bottom of the Gare Loch. Was he referring to the intakes or to the funnel doors, but it does seem to validate Lt Lanes version of events. Lt Singer seems to suggest that the Control Room door was wired up the wrong way.

The intakes were undeniably open when the submarine was diving, this was observed by the divers and seen once the submarine was raised. But if they had been left open by the crew, they would have closed once the hydraulic pressure collapsed. This could have been due to the hydraulic pump losing power by emersion in water or when the batteries ran out of power. As the submarine had settled in an upright position the springs or the weight of the covers would have closed the intakes.

The fact that the salvers had a lot of trouble closing the intakes substantiates the waxing proposal. If the valve was open and hydraulic pressure was keeping them open, the pressure would be removed on sinking or shortly thereafter and the intakes would have shut under the weight of the cover. The oil would have stayed waxed, it would have taken quite aggressive heating to reverse the waxing process. The salvors had to cut the pipes and use hydraulic jacks to close the intakes, maybe this forced out the 'wax'.

Lt Cdr Herbert turned K13 towards the head of the Gare Loch and ordered "Diving Stations". As the submarine prepared to submerge, he walked aft along the superstructure to pass the order down the open engine room hatch. When he got to the Control Room, he took the periscope and ordered, "Dive to 20 feet". Almost immediately, personnel in the Control Room realised that something had gone wrong. The depth gauges showed that the vessel was sinking far too quickly and a report was received that the Boiler Room was flooding. More worryingly, there was a sudden increase in the air pressure. This shows that the Boiler Room / Turbine Room bulkhead had failed, failed almost as soon as the boat started to submerge.

The accident to K13 was undoubtedly caused by the air intakes being open. This explains the flooding of the Boiler Room but it fails to make clear how the Turbine and Motor Rooms flooded and flooded so quickly. Even if the ERA, who came through the air lock, had not clipped the door, it should have held back the rising water. The hatches opened inward, against the air pressure of the closed Boiler Room, or in this case, the pressure of the water, and this would have held the hatches even more tightly shut. Very soon after the boat went under water, Lt Cdr Herbert was of the opinion that the bulkheads aft of the Boiler Room had already collapsed and the compartments had flooded and the men in them drowned.

The internal bulkheads were designed to withstand a rather modest pressure of 15 lb/in^2, normal atmospheric pressure. In normal operation these bulkheads should not see anything above this, the pressure hull took the sea pressure. At a depth of approximately 55 ft the pressure on the bulkhead would be 25 lb/in^2. This was a very a modest overload and it is extremely unlikely that the bulkhead would have burst, collapsed or distorted. But as stated above, the evidence shows that the bulkhead failed at 20 ft. The Boiler Room / Turbine Room bulkhead must have failed, there is no other way the aft compartments could have flooded or flooded so quickly and it explains the rapid rise in air pressure in the Control Room, as the rising sea water forced the air from aft through the voice pipes into the Control Room.

To support this argument, it is noteworthy that the for'd Boiler Room bulkhead, between the Boiler Room and the Midships Torpedo Room, was subjected to the same pressure and didn't collapse. Leakage past cable glands pipes increased and the water level in the Torpedo Room rose at about 2 ft an hour, it was pumped out at intervals with the electric bilge pump. More importantly, Professor Hillhouse didn't mention any bulkhead rupture or distortion once he examined the vessel after she was raised. Interestingly he saw fit to mention the open vents.

Cox'n Moth, who became Cox'n of K14, wrote in his 'War Diaries' that when K13 was raised, the four air intakes to the indicating signifying room were all open, and the Boiler Room door had burst open. He presumably heard this while standing by K14, which was also being built by Fairfield at the time. This is crucial, there must have been a major failure of the Boiler Room / Turbine Room bulkhead for the aft compartments to flood and flood so quickly.

When the bulkhead failed, the aft compartments were rapidly flooded. Air was forced fwd, through the voice pipes quickly followed by water. The three isolation valves on voice pipes, from the stern compartments to the Control Room, were shut off very quickly. However, before this could be done, a jet of water from one of the pipes sprayed the switchboard. This caused several short circuits, which in turn, blew fuses and started a fire in the cables, which rapidly filled the Control Room with white choking smoke.

The voice pipes in the Turbine Room must have been at least 5 ft above the deck level, signifying a rapid and catastrophic flood. This rise in pressure may have shored up the Boiler Room / Midships Torpedo Room bulkhead, the leak rate notably increased when the pressure was released during the rescue operation.

It doesn't seem unreasonable to assume that once the ERA evacuated the Boiler Room and announced that it was flooding via the intakes, that someone would have moved the intake valve lever between the open and closed positions in an attempt to close the intakes. The bulkhead may well have failed when the operator had the lever in the open position.

The submarine came to rest on the bottom of the loch in 65 ft of water, with a slight list to port and an inclination of about 4° up by the bow.

One has to ask if the number of personnel onboard had any effect on the outcome of the accident. The boat was undoubtedly overweight, by some 40%, regarding the number of personnel. It had dived with that number on board, in fact two more in the morning and surfaced without a problem. There is a reported case of a K-class submarine diving with its funnels raised and although the Boiler Room flooded the submarine surfaced. In K13s case once the boat began to flood, the number of personnel onboard, certainly lessened the leeway, and made any chance of recovery improbable.

Undoubtedly K13 sank because it dived with the air intakes opened but there is a strong and robust case to be made that it was outside the control of the crew.

There is no record of an inspection report once the boat was raised.

CHAPTER 6

CONCLUSIONS

By any measure the Board of Inquiry's findings were unsound. Their reasoning still appears illogical and as a result I feel their conclusions are indefensible. Their findings give the impression that the Board had a preconceived idea of the cause of the accident and therefore, the outcome of the investigation had to corroborate this, essentially human fault was to blame.

Not a single technical expert was called or questioned, nor did they consider the possibility of any mechanical failure being the cause of the accident. This is very evident in the fact that they didn't explore the Naval surveyor's explanation of the vent not operating correctly or Mr Skinner's explanation of the vent wiring. Surely these were both crucial topics, directly linked to the sinking of the submarine

The fact that the Board didn't pursue these points, along with many other instances mentioned in the previous chapters and, not forgetting, the unasked questions, call into question the Board's competency and by inference, Lt Lane's guilt. The prime exhibit was still under water making whatever evidence it might hold unavailable to the Board. I also believe that they should have taken cognisance of the K-Class problematic history. There was also the issue of the unasked questions and the inconsistencies shown in some of the evidence statements. None of the Board members were engineers themselves. This could have been of some relevance and it's certainly open to conjecture. Lack of technical knowledge must have limited their understanding of the situation to some degree.

Apart from this, the Board failed to address two major points in their inquiry. Firstly, they failed to recognise the significance of the flickering indicator light and they didn't explore the confusing and inconsistent statements on this subject. The flickering light showed that the intake covers moved, the only way this could have happened is that the valve must have been moved from the open position. Secondly, they didn't consider the possibility of a material failure in the aft Boiler Room bulkhead. Failure of this bulkhead is the only possible explanation of how the stern of the submarine could have flooded and flooded so quickly. The essential fact is that this happened at 20', hardly a serious over pressurisation and the flooding of the stern was the reason the submarine sank.

Why the Board didn't pursue these subjects is open to speculation. It can't be emphasised enough that Lt Lane ensured that the valve had been closed and that he had no control whatsoever over the aft bulk, and it was this failure which ultimately caused the fatal flooding. The fact they failed to explain both these points must surely be viewed as major omission.

In conclusion, I believe the previous chapters clearly present ample proof to show that crew operated the valve to close the intakes and this makes a robust case to call the Board's verdict into question. Added to this, there are several striking similarities between the K2 incident, as detailed in the previous chapter, and the K13 sinking. These must cast further doubt on the Board's findings.

Without a doubt it is my belief that the Board's findings and its conclusion were not only wrong, I strongly feel that the members of the board were guilty, wilfully or not, of dereliction of duty. For the Board to conclude that Lt Lane was solely responsible for the accident after an extremely inadequately executed inquiry, in which they didn't invest more than a few hours, is questionable at least. The inquiry raised more questions than it answered any and perhaps there was more at stake than either the Navy or Fairfield were willing to be made public. Sadly, Lt Lane had no control over the outcome of the inquiry, nor could he defend himself against the blame which was conveniently levelled against him as he tragically died in the sinking of the K13. The verdict unjustly tarnished his reputation and had the consequence of leaving his family without an income, as the verdict, essentially blaming him for the loss of the submarine, denied his wife from claiming a pension from the Royal Navy. It was only by the intervention of

Lt Lane's father, an Admiral, that his widow managed to secure a small income.

While other books have been written about the K13 accident, I believe this book is the first that openly questions the Board's findings. Whilst I accept all this happened a little over a century ago, I do not feel that that is sufficient reason not to re-examine this case. I am confident that the alternative accident scenario, as described in the previous chapter, presents an accurate and persuasive argument in favour of a different series of events. It is a robust, truthful, fact-based account of the accident, which I believe is unquestionably correct.

Truth is, perhaps more a matter of perspective than an actual reality, this is a story that deserves to be told. Maybe a little unrealistically, I would like to think that the result of this book will be that the Board's findings will be officially re-examined. But, regardless of the outcome, I would like to think, at least, I've stated Lt Lane's case, and that has been my main aim from the day I started working on this untold story.

CHAPTER 7

EPILOGUE

On 11th November 1920, the Admiralty granted permission for the Captain of Fort Blockhouse to erect a monument to K13 in the Faslane Cemetery; this would be funded by the Fort Blockhouse Canteen Fund. The memorial to the Fairfield workers lost on K13 was unveiled on 25th November 1922 in

Elder Park, Govan.

K13 monument Faslane

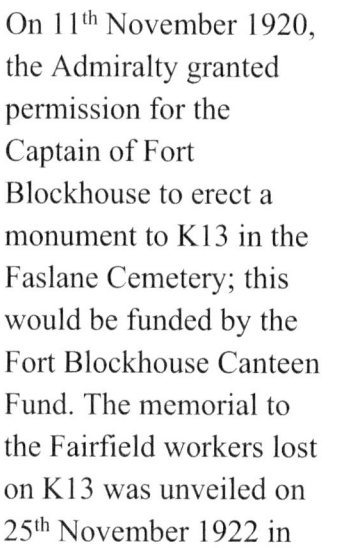

During 1928 concern was raised about the state of the Faslane memorial, primarily that the names were very difficult to read. The original sculptor, Robert Grey of Glasgow, recommended 'leading the names which would cost £27 and last

K13 monument Elder Park Glasgow

forever'. It was decided that this would be the best solution to the problem.

On 29th January 1962 Sydney Glazebrook and K13 survivor Joseph Swift (Telephonist) took part in wreath laying at Elder Park. The Navy had been holding a small remembrance service at the Faslane cemetery for a number of years. In January 1963 the Squadron Padre, Rev AWE Bancroft MA, conducted service which was attended by 26 Navy men who had travelled from

Mr Sidney Glazebrooke of London (left), A.B. gunner on the K.13, and Mr Joseph Swift of Motherwell, a telegraphist on the submarine with the wreath.

The Gareloch tragedy of submarine K13

Beeching!

"He's a very ingenious man and he'll always find a way, but he's not telling anyone that in case it might become overcrowded."

Was it by train? D Beeching usually catches the 8.58 a.m. from East Grinstead (Sussex), but a station official said to-day "We didn't see him."

FOOTNOTE—Trains from East Grinstead were running normally to-day.

EXACTLY 45 years ago to-day the crew of the then largest submarine in the world — the K13 — were trapped many fathoms down in the near-freezing water of the Gareloch — the start of a tragedy that was to shake a world at war.

And to-day in Glasgow two of the men who survived remembered their 31 comrades — seven civilians and the rest Navymen — as they laid a wreath in the shape of a submarine on the

"Evening Times" reporter

memorial outside Old Govan Pres Church.

One of the pair, Mr Sidney Glazebrooke, told me—"This is the realisation of a dream.

"TERRIBLE DAY"

"We have waited all these years to pay this respect and remember that terrible day."

And the other survivor, Mr Joseph Swift, 63, of Catherine Street, Motherwell, nodded in silent agreement.

Rothesay.

In January 1964, crew members of the recently commissioned HMS/M Osiris attended the Service for K13, at the Memorial, in the Faslane Cemetery, Incidentally HMSM Osiris (S13) was the first RN submarine to use 13 as a pennant number since the ill-fated K13.

In January 1965 it was reported that a naval party from HMS Maidstone, 'once again', paid tribute to those lost on K13 in a ceremony held at the Faslane cemetery

On the 50th anniversary in 1967, a group of men from the Depot ship HMS Maidstone paid tribute to the crew and passengers of K13. This was the last time the Royal Navy was involved.

There is a memorial to K13 in Australia. It was unveiled in 1961 by the widow of Charles Albert Harry Freestone, a survivor of K13, who had met Sidney Glazebrook in Portsmouth before leaving for Australia. After leaving the Royal Navy he immigrated to Australia and developed the prosperous business of C. A. Freestone Pty. Ltd, in

The K13 Memorial at Carlingford Australia

Parramatta. The Parramatta district reminded him of Chelmsford where he was born. He set aside a part of the land he owned on Pennant Hills Road, Carlingford in 1956 for the memorial but unfortunately died before he could realise his dream.

In the early 1980s the Chairman of the Scottish Branch, John Jamieson, met Sydney Glazebrook at an International Submariners meeting in Germany. Sydney had expressed his worry that no-one would remember the crew of Submarine K13 after he 'crossed the bar'. It was therefore decided that the Scottish Branch would continue to remember the accident and Sydney was reassured that the Branch would continue to attend the memorial. Over the years Sydney made many visits to the Faslane Cemetery to commemorate the crew and Fairfield personnel lost on that day. His last visit to the cemetery was on 29th January 1980. In an interview with the local newspaper he said:

'Myself and 3 others made a promise and resolution in Portsmouth that we would, as long as possible, visit the graves of our friends each year on the 29th January.

On one occasion, I walked seven miles to Faslane (from Helensburgh Station) carrying a wreath in two feet of snow, arriving at the cemetery after dark and climbing over the locked gate to get in. I then plodded my way back to Helensburgh and slept for a few hours in a shelter on the sea front'.

The West of Scotland Branch of the Submarine Old Comrades Association was formed in August 1986 and WO George Barras, a founder member, was asked by the Central Lancashire, West of Scotland and Scotland Falkirk Branches of the Submarine Old Comrades Association, to arrange the K13 Memorial Service. This service was conducted by Rev Anthony Puder assisted by Rev Ian Rutherford & Rev David Lacey. After the ceremony attendees were entertained at the WOs & SRs Mess. This was the start of the K13 Service that we know today, at this time the Branch meetings were held in the Masonic Halls, visitors attending were accommodated in the Base. Visitors would attend the meeting on the Friday night, drinks in the Mess on the

Saturday then the Memorial service on the Sunday. Three years later, on the 21st January 1990, the first dedicated K13 service was held at St John's Church Faslane. After, the service attendees then went to the Faslane Cemetery. It was during this weekend that the Branch Chairman, Jim McMaster, suggested to a committee member that they should explore the possibility of holding a dinner on the Saturday night. At the Branch meeting on 17th September 1999, which was then held in the Masonic Halls in Helensburgh, the Social Secretary reported that the cost of the K13 Dinner would be £22:50; this would include reception with drinks wine etc.

Over the years the weekend has grown both in numbers attending and the organisations they represent.

The weekend starts late Friday afternoon with visitors arriving at the Base's South Gate. They are then issued with cabin keys, Base passes and the programme for the weekend's activities. All visitors are invited to attend the Friday evening meeting of the West of Scotland Branch. On completion of the meeting Cdr.SubFlot gives a talk on the current state of the Submarine Service. After this, attendees retire to Kennedy's Bar.

After breakfast on Saturday morning a coach leaves the Base for the Memorial Service and wreath laying at Elder Park, Govan. The first visit to Elder Park was made in 2011 by six West of Scotland Branch members.

During the afternoon visits are arranged to the Ship Control Trainer and a visit to a submarine, should one be available.

The evening's festivities start around 1800 with the Punch Reception, before the formal dinner. At the end of the meal attendees retreat to Kennedy's Bar for a little well deserved refreshment.

On Sunday morning a service is held in Base Church, St Johns. After this a Memorial Service is held in the Faslane Cemetery, also respects are paid at the grave of Commander Goodhart, which is a short distance away. Attendees then return to WO and SRs Mess for a buffet lunch. In 2017, for the first time, during the afternoon there was a short service and the 'casting of a wreath' from a fleet tender at the actual accident position.

The Centennial year saw the largest commemoration ever and one can't help but feel that Sidney Glazenbrook would be pleased with the way the K13 Memorial Service has developed over the years. He believed the living owe it to those who no longer can speak, to tell their story for them and I would like to think this is what the weekend does.

On 20 September 2019, veterans and serving submariners joined members of the local community on Wednesday to witness the unveiling of a plinth to mark the sinking of the Submarine K13 at

Helensburgh's outdoor museum in Colquhoun Square. Senior Royal Navy Officers were in attendance, including Commodore (Cdre) Jim Perks, the Commanding Officer of the Faslane Submarine Flotilla.

The plinth was commissioned by the West of Scotland Branch of the Submariners Association the plinth is topped by a bronze sculpture which shows the Gareloch, Submarine K13 and the Submariners Association Crest. On the plinth is an engraving which tells the story of the sinking of K13.

Before the unveiling, Commander Bob Seaward, OBE RN Retired, the President of the West of Scotland Branch, explained how the plinth is a link connecting the town and its residents to the Naval Base and the submarines based there. He thanked everyone involved in the design and creation of the exhibit. He also gave thanks to Argyll and Bute Council for approving the exhibit and for matching the funding which was raised by selling Submariners Association pins and from donations from serving submariners.

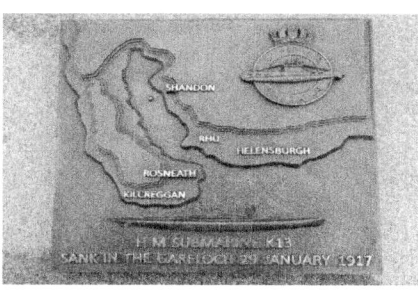

Jim McMaster, the National Chairman of the Submariners Association read the words engraved on the plinth before he officially unveiled the plinth. He said: "As the National Chairman of the Submariners Association I was delighted and honoured to be invited to unveil the K13 plinth in Colquhoun Square, Helensburgh. This latest exhibit to the town's open-air museum is a beautifully crafted reminder, not only of the tragic accident and subsequent loss of life, but also a tribute to an immense rescue operation. The K13 incident is an important and integral part of the town's history."

References

The Royal Naval Submarine Service 1901-1918
 Richard Mackay M.A, B.A.(HONS)

A Precarious Existence. British Submariners in World War One
Richard Mackay MA, BA, (HONS)

British submarine policy 1853-1918
Michael Wynford Dash

K Class Submarines   Don Everitt

K Class Submarine Notes   David Pigget

K 13 Centennial Papers   Gerry McFeely

The Hillhouse Report   Professor P Hillhouse

Early Royal Navy Submariner Training Barrie K Downer,

A paper by J Foster Petree MIMECH.E. MRINA that was
published in Marine Engineer and Naval Architect; Recalling K
13, in which he highlights certain inconsistencies in the Hillhouse
Report and Everitt's description of the K 13 accident.

Oscar Moth War Diaries

Tam Ney Recollections
Clyde Weather Reports from January 1917

Also by the Author

Polaris: The History of the UK's Submarine Force
ISBN 978 0 7524 5177 0

Around the Gareloch and Rosneath Peninsular
ISBN: 978-0-7524-2106-3

HM Naval Base Clyde
978-0-7524-6480-0

HMS Defiance
ISBN: 978-0-7523-3758-3

HMS Dolphin: Gosport's Submarine Base
ISBN: 978-0-7524-2113-1

Gareloch and Rosneath (Pocket Images)
ISBN: 978-1-8458-8402-4

Rosneath and Gareloch: Then and Now
ISBN: 978-0-7524-2389-0

Submariners News: The Peculiar Press of the Underwater Mariner
ISBN: 978-0-7524-5793-2

Submariners: Real Life Stories from the Deep
ISBN: 978-0-7524-2809-3

The Clyde Submarine Base: Images of Scotland
ISBN: 978-0-7524-1657-1

Old Garelochhead & the Rosneath Peninsular
ISBN: 1840330600

Printed in Great Britain
by Amazon

84081936R00139